STEVEN GERRARD

FIFTY DEFINING FIXTURES

STEVEN GERRARD

FIFTY DEFINING FIXTURES

Tony Matthews

AMBERLEY

First published 2015

Amberley Publishing
The Hill, Stroud
Gloucestershire, GL5 4EP

www.amberley-books.com

British Library Cataloguing in Publication Data.
A catalogue record for this book is available from the British Library.

ISBN 978 1 4456 4259 8 (print)
ISBN 978 1 4456 4269 7 (ebook)

Typesetting and Origination by Amberley Publishing.
Printed in the UK.

Contents

Statistics

Personal Information

Full name: Steven George Gerrard
Date of birth: 30 May 1980
Place of birth: Whiston, Merseyside
Playing positions: right-back, right-wing, midfield (various)
Schools: St Michael's Primary (Huyton); Cardinal Heenan High (West Derby, Liverpool)
Teams/clubs: Whiston Juniors (1987), Denburn Park Boys' Club (1988), Liverpool Anfield Academy/School of Excellence (aged eight, August 1988), Liverpool Schoolboys (August 1991–May 1996); Liverpool (apprentice/semi-professional, May 1996; professional, November 1997–May 2015); LA Galaxy (May 2015); also played for England at U21 and senior levels.

Appearances/Goals

Season	PL	FAC	FLC	Europe	Others	Totals
1998/99	12/0	0/0	0/0	1/0	0/0	13/0
1999/2000	29/1	2/0	0/0	0/0	0/0	31/1
2000/01	33/7	4/1	4/0	9/2	0/0	50/10
2001/02	28/3	2/0	0/0	15/1	0/0	45/4
2002/03	34/5	2/0	6/2	11/0	1/0	54/7
2003/04	34/4	3/0	2/0	8/2	0/0	47/6
2004/05	30/7	0/0	3/2	10/4	0/0	43/13
2005/06	32/10	6/4	1/1	12/7	2/1	53/23
2006/07	36/7	1/0	1/1	12/3	1/0	51/11
2007/08	34/11	3/3	2/1	13/6	0/0	52/21
2008/09	31/16	3/1	0/0	10/7	0/0	44/24
2009/10	33/9	2/1	1/0	13/2	0/0	49/12

2010/11	21/4	1/0	0/0	2/4	0/0	24/8
2011/12	18/5	6/2	4/2	0/0	0/0	28/9
2012/13	36/9	1/0	1/0	8/1	0/0	46/10
2013/14	34/13	3/1	2/0	0/0	0/0	39/14
Overall	497/117	41/15	30/9	128/41	4/1	702/138

Representative honours: England: 4 U21 caps (one goal); 114 full caps (21 goals)

(details correct Febuary 2015)

Club Honours (Liverpool)

Winners' Medals:

- FA Cup: 2001, 2006
- League Cup: 2001, 2003, 2012
- FA Community Shield: 2006
- UEFA Champions League: 2005
- UEFA Cup: 2001
- UEFA Super Cup: 2001, 2005

Runners-Up Medals:

- Premier League: 2001/02, 2008/09, 2013/14
- FA Cup: 2012
- League Cup: 2005
- FA Community Shield: 2002
- FIFA World Club Championship: 2005
- UEFA Champions League: 2007

Individual Awards

- Ballon d'Or Bronze Award: 2005
- UEFA Club Footballer of the Year: 2005
- FWA Footballer of the Year: 2009
- FWA Tribute Award: 2013
- PFA Players' Player of the Year: 2006
- PFA Young Player of the Year: 2001
- PFA Fans' Player of the Year: 2001, 2009
- England Player of the Year Award: 2007, 2012
- PFA Team of the Year: 2001, 2004, 2005, 2006, 2007, 2008, 2009, 2014
- Liverpool top goalscorer: 2004/05, 2005/06, 2008/09

- UEFA Euro Team of the Tournament (1): 2012
- UEFA Team of the Year: 2005, 2006, 2007
- FIFA/FIFPro World XI: 2007, 2008, 2009
- ESM Team of the Year: season 2008/09
- Goal of the Season: 2006
- UEFA Champions League final Man of the Match: 2005
- FA Cup final Man of the Match: 2006
- Premier League Player of the Month Award: March 2001, March 2003, December 2004, April 2006, March 2009, March 2014
- ECHO Sports Personality of the Year Award: 2014
- Member of the Order of the British Empire: 2007
- Honorary Fellowship from Liverpool John Moores University: 2008
- BBC Sports Personality of the Year Award (3rd place): 2005
- IFFHS World's Most Popular Footballer: 2006

England International Record

Year	Friendlies		Qualifiers		Competition		Total	
	Apps	Goals	Apps	Goals	Apps	Goals	Apps	Goals
2000	1	0	0	0	1	0	2	0
2001	1	0	5	1	–	–	6	1
2002	2	0	3	1	–	–	5	1
2003	3	1	5	0	–	–	8	1
2004	4	0	2	1	4	1	10	2
2005	3	0	5	1	–	–	8	1
2006	5	1	3	1	5	2	13	4
2007	3	0	8	2	–	–	11	2
2008	5	1	2	1	–	–	7	2
2009	2	0	5	2	–	–	7	2
2010	5	2	3	0	4	1	12	3
2011	0	0	0	0	–	–	0	0
2012	3	0	4	0	4	0	11	0
2013	3	0	5	2	–	–	8	2
2014	3	0	0	0	3	0	6	0
Totals	43	5	50	12	21	4	114	21

Introduction

Once in a generation a football club is blessed with quality player and in Steven Gerrard, Liverpool have just the man.

Wearing the No. 8 shirt for the Anfield Reds, he has been an inspirational captain for a number of years and in 2012 was listed in the top twenty most complete footballers in the world. With power and pace, a certain amount of aggression when required, an effective touch, total commitment and a never-say-die attitude, Stevie G (as he is affectionately known by teammates and supporters alike) has it all, and all these attributes were there for all to see in 2005 when he skippered Liverpool to Champions League glory in Istanbul.

A dynamic midfielder, Steven has collected almost every club medal available during fifteen years in Liverpool's first team and back in 2006 he was awarded an MBE by HRH the Queen. The one piece of silverware that eludes him right now is a special one, a gong for winning the Premier League title. He had also had the honour of captaining England before announcing his retirement from international football in July 2014.

Steve's passion and love for Liverpool football club began when he was spotted by an eagle-eyed scout while playing for local side Whiston Juniors, aged just nine years of age. Switching schools at the age of eleven, he scored a hat-trick in his first game for Cardinal Heenan High in an 8-0 win over Savio High, and as a fourteen-year-old had trials with several clubs, including Manchester United (oh yes he did). A year later he started training at Anfield twice a week before signing as a trainee for Liverpool, having impressed while playing and scoring for Liverpool Boys, starring alongside his close friend to this day – Michael Owen.

Stevie G made excellent progress and was handed a full professional contract by manager Roy Evans, putting pen to paper in the Anfield offices on 5 November 1997, aged seventeen. Within twelve months the young midfield starlet made his senior debut, albeit for barely a minute or so, coming on as a late substitute in place of Vegard Heggem in the Premiership League game against Blackburn Rovers at Anfield on 29 November 1998.

Shortly afterwards Stevie G made his first full appearance for the Reds, lining up in midfield against Tottenham Hotspur at White Hart Lane. Manager Gerard

Houllier gave him the unenviable job of marking the highly-skilled French international David Ginola. He struggled to get to grips with the tricky winger and was taken off in the second half as Liverpool went down 2-1 in front of 36,125 spectators.

Stevie went on to appear in thirteen matches that season, partly due to the injury woes of fellow midfielder Jamie Redknapp, and played his first game in a major European competition, a 1-0 UEFA Cup defeat at the hands of Celta Vigo at Anfield. Four other 'youngsters' from the club's academy played that night – Jamie Carragher, Danny Murphy, Michael Owen and David Thompson. Unfortunately, persistent back and groin problems interrupted Stevie's early career, although he did manage to gain a regular place in Liverpool's starting line-up at the start of the 1999/2000 campaign.

That season proved to be a momentous one for the Whiston-born teenager as he cracked in his first professional goal, a quite superb effort at Anfield against Sheffield Wednesday. He also collected his first red card in Liverpool colours in the Merseyside derby against arch-rivals Everton. Having come on for Robbie Fowler, he was dismissed for a second-half foul on Kevin Campbell. However, at this point England's head coach – the former Liverpool idol Kevin Keegan – was starting to take note, or should that be notes! Surprisingly, Steven never played for England as a schoolboy, but he did make it into the U18 and U21 sides before claiming his first senior cap against Ukraine in May 2000. From there he was selected for Euro 2000, staged in Holland and Belgium, having to settle for just a single substitute appearance in the 1-0 victory over Germany in Charleroi.

At this juncture in his career Steven was now recognised as being by far the complete box-to-box midfielder and he was quite outstanding. He was instrumental when Liverpool completed the unique treble in 2000/01, by winning the Worthington League Cup, the FA Cup and the UEFA Cup final, when he was on the scoresheet in an unforgettable 5-4 UEFA Cup final triumph over the Spanish club Deportivo Alaves. Therefore, it came as no real surprise when Steven – now nicknamed the 'Huyton Hammer' – was duly voted the PFA's Young Player of the Year. Just for the record, in the Premiership in 2000/01 Gerrard started twenty-nine games and made four appearances as a substitute, spending a total of 2,529 minutes on the pitch, helping the Reds finish third and gain a place in the Champions League competition.

In 2001, the tough-tackling Gerrard was asked to visit osteopath Dr Philippe Boixel in France. Every three weeks he travelled over the channel for a day to attend a clinic at the Residence St Pierre, in the town of Laval, 40 miles west of Le Mans. The doctor was contacted by Liverpool boss Gerard Houllier after Gerrard's season had been seriously interrupted by injury, forcing him to miss games for both club and country. Gerrard underwent painful manipulation on his back and spine in an attempt to strengthen his frame. Initially, Gerrard and Houllier had refused to name the doctor involved, but once Steven started to make good progress and gradually win his struggle, Boixel agreed to talk to the media in a rare interview. Dr Boixel, personal trainer to some of the world's best footballers (and other sportsmen), was confident enough to declare: 'There is much work still to be done, but Steven WILL win his battle.'

For quite some time there was no more McDonalds, no burgers, pasta, rice or spuds, and certainly no alcohol for the Liverpool star. But it was all worth it and Gerrard knew after it was all over that he would owe his doctor big time! In fact, the French guru had worked wonders on Steven's back and body, ensuring that his football career would continue for another decade at least.

Virtually 100 per cent fit (again), more memorable and unforgettable moments kept flooding in. Steven started the 2001/02 season by netting his first goal at full international level in the famous 5-1 trouncing of old and bitter rivals Germany in their own backyard. This magnificent victory helped Sven Goran Eriksson's men secure a World Cup place, but sadly an annoying groin injury (not his back) ruled the Liverpool maestro out of the tournament in Japan and South Korea. 'Drat', said Steve, 'I was gutted.'

A rather mixed and unpredictable domestic season followed, but Liverpool and Steven did win a trophy, lifting the Worthington League Cup for the second time in three years by beating Manchester United 2-0 at Cardiff's Millennium Stadium, with Steven scoring the game's first goal.

By the start of the 2003/04 campaign, Steven had firmly established himself as Liverpool's on-field leader in the No. 8 shirt; it came as no real surprise (to anyone in fact) when manager Gerard Houllier handed him the captain's armband in place of centre-back Sami Hyypiä. The decision to make him team skipper proved such a success that within six months Stevie G led out England against Sweden in the absence of David Beckham. Sadly the result in Gothenburg's Ullevi Stadium wasn't a good one as the hosts won 1-0, courtesy of a goal by the pony-tailed Zlatan Ibrahimovic.

Around this time things were bubbling at Anfield for both Steven and Liverpool. There was a great deal of optimism within the club and although there were clear reports that Chelsea had offered £20 million for Steve, which he waved aside, the team itself could only manage a fifth-place finish in the Premiership.

Players and supporters alike duly joined forces with Steve, who enjoyed the greatest night of his Liverpool career when, on 5 May 2005, under new boss Rafael Benítez, the Scouser from Whiston gleefully lifted the club's fifth European Cup on a memorable night in Turkey. Having already brought Liverpool back from the brink of elimination earlier in the competition with a stunning strike against Olympiacos, Steven helped inspire the greatest comeback of all time in Istanbul. No one believed the Reds could overturn AC Milan's 3-0 half-time lead – that is until Stevie G's 54th-minute header reduced the deficit to two. The Reds stormed forward, scored twice more to draw level and then went on to win the star prize on penalties. What a night!

Steve's heroics earned him the title of UEFA's Most Valuable Player, as well as a nomination for the prestigious Ballon d'Or award. He would subsequently come third in the latter, behind Ronaldinho and fellow countryman Frank Lampard, of Chelsea.

In the months that followed that epic final, Liverpool's 'Captain Fantastic' signed a new four-year contract at Anfield to put an end to speculation about a possible move to Chelsea. He never really wanted to go there, did he? With his future on Merseyside secured, Steven went on to enjoy his most impressive season to date, that of 2005/06, when he scored twenty-three goals in fifty-three games for the Reds. He was also crowned PFA Player of the Year, being the first Liverpool star to receive that coveted award since winger John Barnes back in 1988.

The 2005/06 campaign culminated in another FA Cup final win in Cardiff. West Ham United provided the opposition, and if the 1953 game at Wembley between Blackpool and Bolton is remembered as being the Stanley Matthews final, then the 2006 encounter will surely go down as Stevie G's day. The midfielder twice beat goalkeeper Shaka Hislop, his second strike a dramatic equaliser in the dying moments to take the well-contested game into extra time and, ultimately, to penalties. This stunning 35-yard volley, which made it 2-2, was voted BBC Match of the Day's Goal of the Season. And rightly so. Gerrard – who's has now played in just about every outfield position for Liverpool – had scored in four major cup finals, something no English-based player had ever done before he achieved the feat in 2006.

During the summer of 2006, at the age of twenty-six, Steven featured in his first World Cup. After playing well and scoring twice in the group stages, he was unfortunately one of three players who missed from the spot in the quarter-final penalty shoot out defeat by Cristiano Ronaldo's Portugal.

Steven – fit and raring to go – returned from Germany for another eventful domestic season in which he broke Ian Rush's European Cup goalscoring record, his smart header against PSV Eindhoven being his fifteenth in the competition, one more than the legendary Welsh striker.

In December 2006, and by now the idol of the Anfield Kop, Steven was awarded an MBE, which he later collected from her majesty the Queen at Buckingham Palace. If all this wasn't enough to cope with, the season ended with yet another European Cup final appearance, and once again Liverpool's opponents were AC Milan. This time, however, the night ended in heartbreak for everyone associated with the Reds as the Italian side won 2-1 in Athens.

Back on the international front, there was despair in November 2007 when Steven skippered his country in a 3-2 defeat by Croatia at the new Wembley Stadium – ending both England's hopes of qualifying for Euro 2008 and Steven McClaren's reign as national team manager. Disappointingly, Steven and Liverpool also finished the season without a single piece of silverware despite a twenty-one-goal haul from the Reds' midfielder, who formed an irrepressible partnership with Spanish striker, and new record signing, Fernando Torres.

Now clearly a bona fide legend of the British game, Steven reached a milestone of 100 goals for Liverpool with a powerful right-footed free-kick against PSV Eindhoven in October 2008, at the same time joining an elite band of sixteen other Anfield legends to achieve the feat. This wonderful strike was one of twenty-four goals scored by Steven during the 2008/09 campaign – a personal record that earned him the Football Writers' Player of the Year award for the first time.

Sadly, his excellent goal-tally wasn't quite enough to secure an elusive Premier League winners' medal. Despite Liverpool mounting their best challenge since 1989/90, they fell just short in second place behind rivals Manchester United, who crossed the line on the penultimate weekend of the thirty-eight-match campaign to win the title by ninety points to eight-six. All this persuaded Stevie G – now the pride of Merseyside by a country mile – to once again commit his future to the club by agreeing a two-year extension to his contract, thus tying him to Anfield until he was thirty-three years of age.

Another frustrating and disappointing term followed, although Steven still plundered twelve goals as Liverpool finished seventh in 2009/10 behind Chelsea. The midfielder also made his 500th first-class appearance for the club in the 0-0 Premiership draw with Blackburn Rovers at Ewood Park in December 2009.

On the international front, an injury to Rio Ferdinand meant it was Steven who led England in the World Cup in South Africa in the summer of 2010. He scored in the opening group game draw with USA, played well in the 0-0 draw with Algeria and the 1-0 win over Slovenia, but like his teammates, was disappointed to say the least when Germany upset the apple cart by winning a last sixteen encounter 4-1 in Bloemfontein.

On his return to Anfield, Steven found that an awful lot had altered. Manager Rafael Benítez had gone, replaced, for the time being at least, by Roy Hodgson (later to become England boss). Over the coming months the ownership of the club would change following a courtroom battle between Messrs. Tom Hicks and George Gillett and newcomers NESV.

Niggling injuries meant that Steven was often helpless in assisting the club out on the pitch during the 2010/11 season as the Hodgson revolution went awry, although Steve's ability to turn in a handful of 'Roy of the Rovers' performances was still evident. He bagged a brace, albeit to no avail, in a 3-2 Premiership defeat at Old Trafford, and with Liverpool trailing he struck a late hat-trick to ensure a 3-1 home Europa League Group K victory over Napoli – after initially being rested! It's amazing what a break can do.

Unfortunately Liverpool entered 2011 in a rather desperate and worrying state and as a result, the club's new owners, John Henry and Tom Werner, between them decided to install as manager the only man with a claim against Steven for the title of Liverpool's greatest ever player – former player Kenny Dalglish.

Despite a few more tedious injury problems, Steven went out and ensured there were some happy memories during Dalglish's sixteen-month tenure. In February

2012, he proudly led the Reds out at the new Wembley for the first time, and though he missed a penalty in the shoot-out against Cardiff City, Liverpool eventually triumphed, enabling Steven to climb the steps to the Royal Box and lift the Carling League Cup.

Just a few weeks after this success, Steven did something which, even without any of the above, would have made him a legend in the minds of Liverpool fans; he scored a hat-trick in a 3-0 win over Everton at Anfield, a feat that hadn't been achieved since September 1935 when Fred Howe netted a four-timer in a 6-0 home victory over their Merseyside rivals.

In 2011, Stevie G started the Steven Gerrard Foundation with the aim of supporting children's charities in and around Merseyside, something that is still going strong today.

The 2011/12 season ended with news that new England boss Hodgson had named Steven as his permanent captain ahead of Euro 2012. Although it was the greatest of tournaments for England – they went out on penalties at the quarter finals stage to Italy – Stevie G flourished. He assisted in the three goals his country scored and was generally regarded as being England's star performer overall.

In July 2013, Liverpool announced that Steven had signed an extension to his contract, meaning he would remain at Anfield until his retirement (all things considered). In finding the back of the net with a penalty against Newcastle United at St James' Park in October 2013, he reached the landmark of 100 goals in the Premier League – only the 12th Liverpool player to achieve such a feat. Quite brilliant, especially for a midfielder!

The heartbeat of an unexpected title challenge under Brendan Rodgers in 2013/14, and having been asked to drop into a new deeper role in front of the back four, Steven played very well during the campaign which saw the Reds finish second in the Premiership behind champions Manchester City, the title going to the Etihad Stadium on the final day.

Soon after the season was over, Steven teamed up with the England party and set off for Brazil and the 2014 World Cup. Again named as skipper on football's greatest stage, he had four of his Anfield colleagues for company – Jordan Henderson, Glen Johnson, Raheem Sterling and Daniel Sturridge, plus Adam Lallana and Rickie Lambert who would soon join him at Anfield – but unfortunately Roy Hodgson's Three Lions failed to produce the goods, losing to Italy and Luis Suarez's Uruguay and drawing with Costa Rica in their group, therefore failing to qualify for the knockout stage. The game against Costa Rica proved to be the final time Steven pulled on an England shirt. He announced his retirement from international football having collected 114 full caps, just one less than David Beckham's record haul of 115 for an outfield player.

Prior to the start of the 2014/15 season, Stevie G said that Liverpool, given the breaks, 'could surprise a few teams, both in the Premiership and Champions League, and that hopes were high at Anfield'. Remember, they'd never won the Premiership title since the 1992 League competition was introduced and still haven't, as things simply did not go according to plan out on the pitch during the first half of the campaign. Results were hit and miss, and to cap it all Liverpool were dumped out of the Champions League at the group stage, meaning they had to enter the Europa League. However, progress was made to the League Cup semi-finals (only to be beaten over two legs by Chelsea) and after knocking out Bournemouth and Bolton, the Reds were looking good in the FA Cup.

With half a season remaining, on New Year's Day in 2015 Stevie G stunned the world of football by saying that he would be leaving Anfield when his contract ended in May.

The Reds' captain revealed that he would not come into direct competition with Liverpool: 'I will play for LA Galaxy in the MLS', he said. With a heavy heart, Gerrard described the decision to leave Anfield as the 'toughest of my life', but chose to make it when he did to avoid speculation about his future. Explaining his decision, he said:

This has been the toughest decision of my life and one which both my family and I have agonised over for a good deal of time. I am making the announcement now so that the manager and the team are not distracted by stories or speculation about my future. Liverpool Football Club has been such a huge part of all our lives for so long and saying goodbye is going to be difficult, but I feel it's something that's in the best interests of all involved, including my family and the club itself. I'm going to carry on playing and although I can't confirm at this stage where that will be, I can say it will be somewhere that means I won't be playing for a competing club and will not therefore be lining up against Liverpool – that is something I could never contemplate. My decision is completely based on my wish to experience something different in my career and life and I also want to make sure that I have no regrets when my playing career is eventually over. I can't thank Brendan [Rodgers], the owners and everyone at the club enough for how they've handled this and I am leaving on great terms. Also, I would like to thank my teammates and all the staff for their help and continued support. It is a very special place to be part of. It is my sincere hope and wish that one day I can return to serve Liverpool again, in whatever capacity best helps the club. One point that is important to make is that from now until the last kick of the last game of the season, I will be as fully committed to the team as I ever have been and giving everything I have to help Liverpool win games. My final message is for the people who make Liverpool Football Club the greatest in the world – the supporters. It has been a privilege to represent you, as a player and as captain. I have cherished every second of it and it is my sincere wish to finish this season and my Liverpool career on a high.

PREMIER LEAGUE
LIVERPOOL 2 BLACKBURN ROVERS 0
29 November 1998

Liverpool manager Gerard Houllier had not been happy with his team's overall performances during the first twelve weeks of the 1998/99 season. In fact, the Reds were languishing in ninth place in the Premiership after fourteen matches, having recorded only five wins and four draws against five defeats, having also been dumped out of the League Cup by Tottenham. They had crashed 3-1 to Celta Vigo in a UEFA Cup encounter in Spain and – something incomprehensible to many fans – they had lost three games on the bounce at Anfield! Aiming to blood youngsters whenever possible, Houllier opted to include eighteen-year-old Steven Gerrard in his squad for the home game against bottom of the table Blackburn Rovers in late November. Rovers were struggling at the time, having lost five of the previous six League games.

The teenage 'Scouser' was named as a substitute after some exceedingly positive displays in the second XI, not only in recent weeks but also during the previous season when Liverpool finished runners-up, just three points behind Sunderland (49-46) in the Pontins Premier League.

Liverpool (1-4-3-2): James, Heggem (Gerrard), Bjornebye, Babb, Carragher, Staunton (Kvarme), Redknapp, Ince, Fowler, Owen, Berger.
Blackburn (4-4-1-1): Filan, Kenna, Henchoz, Davidson, Dailly, Marcolin, Johnson (Davies), Gallagher, Duff, Dunn, Blake.
Attendance: 41,753

After a splendid 4-2 win away at Aston Villa in their previous Premiership game, Liverpool produced a rather lacklustre opening half-hour against struggling Rovers, but then two goals in quick succession suddenly lifted the gloom that had descended over Anfield. Liverpool midfielder Paul Ince cracked in a stunning 30-yarder in the 30th minute before Michael Owen, with an instinctive piece of quality finishing, made it two nil three minutes and two attacks later.

Let's be frank though ... Liverpool had not played at all well up that point, yet their diehard fans believed they were slowly getting back to some sort of form, hence some hearty chanting from the Kop. Liverpool defended resiliently after going two up, eventually celebrating a hard-earned victory with their first clean sheet in ten matches. After the game, manager Houllier pulled no punches by stating, in no uncertain terms, that it will take quite some time to put things right on the pitch, saying: 'It will be a long process but two League wins in succession gives us all a platform to build on.'

Blackburn fielded virtually a reserve side against Liverpool, as caretaker manager Tony Parkes had no less than eight first-team players sidelined through injury or suspension, including Tim Flowers, Tim Sherwood and Chris Sutton. Ince returned as Liverpool's skipper to add some steel to the midfield engine room. He was in the thick of the action early on, as was Patrik Berger, whose volley was brilliantly saved by John Filan while Jamie Redknapp drove inches over. Steven Staunton was booked for pulling back Rovers' forward Kevin Gallacher a yard outside the box. The free-kick was deflected wickedly wide of David James's far post. At 10 minutes, Nathan Blake fired over from 12 yards and within seconds Damien Johnson headed inches above the angle. At this juncture Liverpool were under pressure.

Blackburn continued to push forward and Liverpool's only effort on goal was a rather weak header by Robbie Fowler. Then Anfield erupted following Ince's magnificent goal. Fowler held the ball up some 30 yards out and, as Ince moved alongside, he laid off a measured pass for the midfielder who took the ball in his stride before smashing it into the net, off Filan's left-hand post, for his fourth goal of the season.

3 minutes later Liverpool went 2-0 ahead and Ince was involved again. His cross from the right found the unmarked Fowler, who half-killed the ball, allowing Owen to fire in a shot that Filan blocked. But the nineteen-year-old striker reacted quickest and found the net from just inside the 6-yard box. Few chances were created up to the interval and in fact nobody dared to suggest that Liverpool, although two goals to the good, had sealed the victory.

During the early stages of the second half, Owen's pace caused Blackburn plenty of problems and three times he threatened to expose a sluggish defence. His best chance came after Fowler had sent him clear, but he pulled his effort well wide and when Christian Dailly's back pass fell short of Filan, the 'keeper narrowly beat Owen to the loose ball. At this stage of the game it was Owen against Blackburn, and a fierce 18-yard effort from the young striker bounced off Filan's chest. Blackburn had nothing to offer now and after Berger had shot over the bar, Steven Gerrard was introduced into the action for his Liverpool debut. He came on for Heggem in the 89th minute and managed to get two touches of the ball before referee Jeff Winter blew the final whistle.

Summing up, Liverpool, despite being 2-0 up, lacked the mental strength to go on and win the game more impressively. There was some smart inter-passing at times, but on the other hand the ball was given away far too easily. If Liverpool had come up against a higher-placed team than Blackburn, the final result may well have been different. Despite all that, Stevie G had got off on a winning note. He made his first start in the senior side at Tottenham six days later, but this time things were somewhat different as Liverpool lost 2-1.

PREMIER LEAGUE
LIVERPOOL 3 EVERTON 2
3 April 1999

Before taking part in his first Merseyside Derby, Steven Gerrard had played in just seven Premiership games (three wins, four defeats) and he had yet to score a goal. When Liverpool took on their near neighbours at Anfield at Easter 1999, Everton were in some sort of trouble, lying just above the relegation zone. They were 16th in the Division and had won only two of their previous thirteen Premiership games. Liverpool meanwhile were sitting in ninth position, in no real danger of demotion or even challenging for a top four finish. Steven was named as a substitute for the game and would enter the action with barely 20 minutes remaining.

Liverpool (4-4-2): James, Heggem (Gerrard), Song, Staunton, Matteo, Berger, McManaman, Redknapp, Ince, Fowler (Riedle), Owen.
Everton (4-4-2): Myhre, Unsworth, Materazzi (Weir), Short, Watson, Ball, Dacourt, Gemmill, Barmby (Jeffers), Branch (Cadamarteri), Campbell.
Attendance: 44,852

There was a minute's silence, impeccably observed, before the start of the game, to mark the 10th anniversary of the Hillsborough disaster, but the noise levels were soon rising!

Everton boss Walter Smith gave senior debuts to new signings Kevin Campbell and Scot Gemmill and it was the visitors who made the best possible start. Steven Staunton headed a long throw into the path of Olivier Dacourt, who was some 30 yards from goal. Connecting fully with the ball, the Frenchman marked his derby debut with a ferocious volley that skimmed off Staunton's head and soared over David James into the top corner. After this the tackling became ferocious. Scott Gemmill was booked for clattering into Robbie Fowler and Michael Ball and Paul Ince were lucky not to follow after two crunching clashes in as many minutes. Then Nicky Barmby was cautioned for sending Jamie Redknapp spinning into the air after 14 minutes. A minute later, Liverpool were level when Marco Materazzi tripped Ince inside the area to concede a penalty.

Fowler netted from the spot, but the Liverpool striker upset quite a few supporters inside the ground after finding the net, falling on all fours to sniff the goal-line in a gesture most onlookers presumed was intended to mock the taunts of Everton supporters over his alleged social habits. Everton fans had taken great delight in goading Fowler during the past two years. It came to a head last season when the Liverpool star made a public denial of drug-taking allegations.

However, as a result of his antics following his spot kick conversion, Fowler faced another run-in with the Football Association, having to appear before the FA to explain his contretemps with Chelsea's Graeme Le Saux, so this was scarcely the brightest way to prepare for the hearing. Liverpool manager Gerard Houllier insisted after the game that the gesture had nothing to do with drugs, but was merely a joke used by French club Metz and introduced to Liverpool players by Rigobert Song, who played for Metz last season.

'It was really nothing', said Houllier. 'Rigobert said they did this at Metz and the players were doing it in training. Robbie was just pretending to eat the grass. I spoke to Robbie about it and also to the referee, and he said he would not be putting it in his report. You can say it was inadvisable in the circumstances, but when your heart is going at 180 beats a minute these things happen. It was certainly not a response to the Everton fans.'

Fowler's equaliser certainly raised the temperature inside the ground, and as Liverpool buckled down and began to take control of the game, their first win over their Merseyside neighbours in ten meetings looked a distinct possibility when, in the 21st minute, 'man of the moment' Fowler gave his side the lead. Everton goalkeeper Thomas Myhre produced a fingertip save to deny Steven McManaman before flicking the subsequent corner from Patrik Berger onto Fowler, who headed in at the far post. This time there was no attempt to taunt the fans ... it was Liverpool 2 Everton 1.

Everton hit back and Staunton fouled Michael Branch, but Materazzi's free-kick, a swerving effort from 25 yards, crashed against James's right-hand post. Then Michael Owen almost made it three for Liverpool, but his snap shot was kept out by Myhre in desperate style. Everton continued to press when the opportunity arose, but Liverpool's defence held firm and, in fact, James was hardly troubled, comfortably collecting two high crosses and dealing with three long-range efforts.

With just 20 minutes remaining, Houllier sent on Steven Gerrard for his first taste of action in a Merseyside Derby, and after Owen and Ince had gone close Berger volleyed in a third goal for Liverpool 8 minutes from time. However, urged on by their fans Everton came again, and with 6 minutes remaining Francis Jeffers reduced the Reds' advantage. Pressed back, Liverpool were now amazingly being forced to hang on, and Danny Cadamarteri could have snatched an improbable equaliser had Gerrard not swept his shot off the line with James stranded. Gerrard then made another goal-line clearance as the second slowly ticked by.

When referee David Elleray finally signalled the end of an exceptionally good contest, a delighted Houllier leapt from the dug-out and punched the air with two fists in near delirium. A victory over Everton meant that much. 'We badly needed the win for the fans,' said Houllier. 'It was a reward for them. We were shakier in the last 10 minutes than in the rest of the match, which was silly. But I hope this will boost our confidence.'

His opposite number, Walter Smith, rued his team's continued struggle for points. He said,

I felt we should have got something out of it. The referee was quick enough to give them a penalty in the first half. And I felt it was a definite spot kick when Danny Cadamarteri was pulled back in the box. We could have had another one too. The result was frustrating and the goals we conceded came from two corners and a penalty. That was very disappointing.

FA CUP, 3RD ROUND
HUDDERSFIELD TOWN 0 LIVERPOOL 2
12 December 1999

This was the earliest FA Cup game Liverpool had ever played in a season and it wasn't an easy one against Steven Bruce's highly efficient League One leaders.

Liverpool, 5th in the Premiership at the time, were favorites to progress into the 4th round and manager Gerard Houllier handed Steven Gerrard his debut in the competition, switching him from midfield to right-back to accommodate Vladimir Smicer who had recovered from injury.

This was certainly a 'banana skin' tie as they say, and Liverpool were taking nothing for granted as the travelled across the Pennines into Yorkshire for a 'Battle of the Roses' encounter.

Huddersfield Town (4-4-2): Vaesen, Jenkins, Gray, Armstrong, Vincent, Sellars, Irons, Gorre, Thornley (Donis), Wijnhard, Stewart (Schofield).
Liverpool (4-4-2): Westerveld, Gerrard (Newby), Hyypiä, Henchoz, Staunton (Matteo), Carragher, Hamann, Smicer (Song), Murphy, Owen, Camara.
Attendance: 23,678

After an excellent encounter, Huddersfield were left cursing their luck for missing no less than a dozen clear-cut chances as Liverpool just about managed to wriggle through to the 4th round. The Terriers dictated play and possession for long periods and if the truth be known they deserved to win, but resilient Liverpool made the most of their limited openings, underlining the fine line between First Division football and the Premiership. Huddersfield were undone by a 36th minute first-half rocket, fired home completely out of the blue by Titi Camara, which was followed a quarter of an hour after half time by left-back Dominic Matteo's excellent finish.

Zipping the ball around with precision and speed, the Terriers had nine strikes on goal to Liverpool's three in the first 45 minutes alone. This was perhaps expected, because Huddersfield's potent attack had already netted thirty-nine goals so far during the season while Liverpool's defence had conceded only fourteen.

Inspired by two talented midfielders – Ben Thornley and thirty-four-year-old Scott Sellars – the Terriers were on the front foot from the kick-off and Liverpool came under severe pressure for the first 15 minutes. Goalkeeper Sander Westerveld saved shots from skipper Kenny Irons and blocked Clyde Wijnhard's one-on-one low chip, both within the space of 60 seconds. But, against the run of play, Camara should have given Liverpool the lead on 10 minutes but somehow screwed an 8-yard shot 4 yards wide.

Michael Owen, who was largely overshadowed by the other three strikers on show, produced one flash of brilliance with a cheeky chip shot, which Nico Vaesen tipped to safety. Westerveld was again in action, saving at the near post from Thornley, but he had centre-back Stephane Henchoz to thank for a timely block on the excellent Dean Gorre. Clearly concerned at the space his back four were allowing their hosts, Liverpool boss Houllier replaced the ageing Steven Staunton with Matteo before the half-hour mark. Virtually straightaway, Vladimir Smicer surged down the right before setting up Camara who netted with a booming shot. While it was against the run of play, this sort of thing happens so often in knockout Cup football.

Credit was due to Huddersfield, who went in search of an equaliser with all guns blazing but were hit hard by a Liverpool counter-attack when Camara, on the half-way line, struck a cross-field ball which fell just behind Dietmar Hamann, but was latched onto by overlapping left-back Matteo. He darted into the box, past Irons, who slipped when preparing to make a challenge, before slamming a left-foot shot under the diving of Nico Vaesen. Owen came alive a little more in the second-half, but poor finishing saw him squander two glorious chances. Steven Gerrard also had to cracks at goal (off target) but generally he had a decent game. Wijnhard was also wasteful for Huddersfield who continued to threaten right until the end and substitute Donis was unlucky with a 79th minute drive, which brought a fine save from Westerveld. The hosts ended the game goalless and with Steven Gerrard having a decent enough game in midfield, Liverpool managed to hold on for an unimpressive win.

INTERNATIONAL FRIENDLY
ENGLAND 2 UKRAINE 0
31 May 2000

The first ever meeting between England and Ukraine was a friendly, played at the old Wembley Stadium back in 2000 – a significant date in English football history for a number of reasons. First of all, Tony Adams' strike for England's second goal, which clinched a 2-0 victory, was in fact the last scored by an Englishman at Wembley before the ground was knocked down and rebuilt, and it was also the Arsenal defender's first goal for England in eleven years.

Manager Kevin Keegan handed a young Steven Gerrard his international debut, 24 hours after his twentieth birthday. He started at right-back and played very well before being forced to limp off in the 81st minute, to be replaced by Kieron Dyer. Keegan, ex-Liverpool of course, said: 'I was impressed', as he widely praised his new starlet for his influence in the game and the way he linked up with David Beckham. Gareth Barry also won his first full cap as substitute, while Alan Shearer was playing his last international on English soil. The opening goal was scored by Anfield teammate Robbie Fowler, who reacted quickest to a rebound from Shearer's powerful header from a corner.

This was the final warm-up game for Keegan's side before the 2000 European Championships, co-hosted by Belgium and Holland. And sadly we all know what happened next: England failed to make the quarter-finals!

England (3-5-2): Martyn, Southgate, Adams, Campbell, Gerrard (Dyer), Beckham, Scholes (Barmby), McManaman, P. Neville (Barry), Shearer, Fowler (Heskey).
Ukraine (4-4-2): Kernozenko (Levytsky), Luzhny, Dimitrulin, Vaschuk, Timoschchyuk, Popov (Vorebey), Kandaurou (Morov), Holokov, Husin, Shevchenko, Rebrov.
Attendance: 55,975

Surprisingly to some, manager Kevin Keegan decided to change his formation to 3-5-2 for this friendly against Ukraine and it paid dividends with a well-earned 2-0 win.

The influential David Beckham almost created an excellent goal after just 6 minutes but his free-kick curled narrowly wide of goalkeeper Vyacheslav Kernozenko's far post. Then Paul Scholes beat the Ukraine's Cuban-born 'keeper with a low drive, only for the ball to strike an upright and fly away to safety with no attacking player around.

After a period of steady, uneventful football, the visitors suddenly burst into life. England's defenders had not been troubled at all but on 10 minutes they had to deal with a tight situation when Andrey Shevchenko threatened and 30 seconds later Serhiy Rebrov almost broke through when Sol Campbell and Gareth Southgate hesitated.

Play was rather scrappy with neither side able to create a worthwhile opening, although Beckham and Shearer both fired in long range shots, alas to no effect, while Rebrov had a fleeting chance at the other end of the field. With barely a minute remaining in the first half England – against the run of play it must be said – scored! Some fans never even saw the goal, having got up and made their way to a bar or tearoom.

Ukraine conceded a corner which was taken by Beckham. He swung over the flag-kick, above a group of near post defenders and onto the head of Shearer, who saw Kernozenko push the ball out, but only as far as Robbie Fowler who was 6 yards, smashing it back high into the net from 3 yards!

England went to the break a goal to the good. But as a unit they hadn't played well, Gerrard, Beckham and Shearer being the only bright spots. Keegan brought on Emile Heskey for Fowler at the start of the second half but it was Ukraine who had the first serious shot after the interval, Nigel Martyn pulling off a very good save to prevent Shevchenko from equalising.

On the hour mark, the lively figure of Scholes appealed unsuccessfully for a penalty, claiming he was brought down inside the box, but the impressive Slovakian referee, Lubos Michel, waved play on, much to the annoyance of the fiery midfielder and a few other England players.

Leeds United's goalkeeper Martyn was having a fine match and he produced another excellent save to deny Shevchenko again as Ukraine hit back strongly. But it was England who struck the next blow when Arsenal's centre-back Tony Adams, up for a left-wing corner taken by Beckham, brought his goal drought to an end in the 68th minute, lashing home a low right-footer from the edge of the penalty area after 'keeper Kernozenko had once more parried a close-range header. The last time Adams scored for his country was back in 1988.

With 15 minutes of the game remaining, Gareth Barry came on for his senior debut, replacing Phil Neville, while Nicky Barmby took over from the industrious Paul Scholes. Before the final whistle, with the Ukraine players tiring rapidly, Heskey had a great chance to make the score 3-0. After facing a one-on-one situation with Kernozenko, the Liverpool striker hit the ball straight at the Ukrainian goalkeeper – a bad miss.

England played with more fluency and commitment in the second half – far better than they did in the first – but something was lacking and manager Keegan and the supporters knew this. Having tried out a few more players and having taken on good opponents, Keegan was obviously pleased with this result. It was Malta next for England in a final preparation game before the real thing on 12 June. They scrambled a 2-1 win (without Stevie G), before it all went sadly wrong in Belgium and the Netherlands, when they lost 3-2 to Portugal and by the same score against Romania, despite beating the foe of Germany.

Stevie G gained his second full cap, coming on as a second-half substitute for buddy Michael Owen against the Germans. He and bustled around during the 30 minutes he was on the pitch and even clattered into his Liverpool teammate Dietmar Hamann. 'I thought I would be booked', said Stevie, 'I was certainly late. I escaped punishment and congratulated Didi after the game.'

LEAGUE CUP SEMI-FINAL 2ND LEG
LIVERPOOL 5 CRYSTAL PALACE 0
(6-2 on aggregate)
24 January 2001

Liverpool had not played at all well in the first leg of their League Cup semi-final against Crystal Palace at Selhurst Park. Producing an under-par performance, they were defeated 2-1 and knew they would have a tough fight on their hands if they were to make it through to the eighth final.

Manager Gerard Houllier, however, argued that Liverpool's position in the Premiership was of far greater importance than their progression in one, two, or even in all of the three major cup competitions. But deep down he knew that another final appearance would be most satisfying, not only himself but for the Anfield supporters who simply loved to celebrate success.

Liverpool (4-4-2): Westerveld, Gerrard (Hamann), Henchoz, Hyypiä, Carragher (Ziege), Smicer (Barmby), Murphy, McAllister, Biscan, Fowler, Litmanen.
Crystal Palace (4-4-2): Kolinko, Austin, Smith, Harrison, Thomson, Rubins (Gray), Rodger, Carlisle (Pollock), Black, Morrison, Forssell (Gregg).
Attendance: 41,854

Not only did Liverpool produce a superb display, as they should have done against a club from a lower division, they could well have won this second-leg encounter with a scoreline of 8, 9 or perhaps 10 nil.

They made the impertinent Clinton Morrison regret the comments he made following the game at Selhurst Park a fortnight earlier, when he had mocked Liverpool's forwards for their inability to convert several clear-cut chances, insisting that if he had received the same service afforded to Michael Owen and Emile Heskey, he would have done far better!

For such impudence, Palace's twenty-one-year-old striker paid dearly, as Liverpool produced a masterclass in attacking football to complete blow away their London challengers with goals from Vladimir Smicer, Danny Murphy (who netted twice), Igor Biscan and Robbie Fowler. Morrison didn't do too much; his best opportunity came early in the second half, and to the delight of the supporters, he miskicked in front of the Kop! Liverpool chief Gerard Houllier had warned Morrison that 'spitting in the air can sometimes result in the need for a handkerchief' and the striker certainly got some stick!

Liverpool qualified for their first cup final in five years with an all-action wonderful performance, and the boss's decision to name Fowler in his starting line-up, despite Emile Heskey having recovered from a thigh injury, was spot on. During the ten weeks prior to this game, Fowler's future at Anfield had been one of uncertainty, but such was the quality of his performance as Liverpool's lone striker against the Eagles, Houllier had to think again before recalling either Heskey or even the injured Owen.

Fowler deservedly found the net in the 89th minute to take his tally to twenty-six goals in thirty-one League Cup appearances, while his overall contribution on the night was very significant. Named as captain, Fowler gathered his teammates into a rugby-scrum huddle before the kick-off, and whatever he said certainly had the desired effect, such was the ferocity of Liverpool's football from the moment the first whistle sounded. A smart one-two involving Jari Litmanen and Murphy ended with the latter's effort being well saved by Palace's Latvian 'keeper Aleksandrs Kolinko. Having shot out of the blocks, it wasn't long before Palace's conceded.

In the 12th minute, Smicer, who had scored Liverpool's late goal at Selhurst Park in the first leg, put his side back into this semi-final with a fine strike. He chased down a wonderful 'inside a full-back' pass from Fowler, held off the foul challenge of Wayne Carlisle before beating Kolinko with a crisp, low drive. 2 minutes later, Liverpool scored again to take an aggregate lead. A wonderfully measured cross from Litmanen found Murphy free on the right-hand side of the Palace penalty area. The midfielder connected brilliantly with his right foot, as he sent a superb volley screaming past Kolinko' left hand. Steven Gerrard was first to congratulate Murphy, whose effort was a certain contender for 'goal of the season'. Under intense pressure, Palace simply had nowhere to go and in the 17th minute found themselves three down. A delightful back-heel by Fowler released Biscan, who moved forward before scoring with a deft right footer.

Palace tried to get forward but found Liverpool's back line impregnable, and in fact the hosts almost scored again halfway through the first half when Gary McAllister almost broke a post in half with a 25-yarder. Then, with the goal at his mercy, Litmanen elected to head Smicer's cross back across goal when it looked easier to find the net! Palace won a free-kick soon afterwards but Tommy Black's effort was tipped over by Sander Westerveld.

Liverpool began the second half as they had the first – on the attack – and in the 51st minute Murphy increased the lead to 4-0 with a fine solo effort that even the Palace fans applauded. To add to their misery, the visitors had goalkeeper Kolinko sent off 7 minutes from time for a foul on Fowler just outside the 18-yard box. The icing was put on top of the Anfield cake in the 89th minute when Fowler deservedly got his goal, converting Murphy's astute pass by slipping the ball under the legs of replacement 'keeper Matt Gregg, who came on for Rubins.

Next up for Liverpool, a meeting with Birmingham City in the final at Cardiff's Millennium Stadium in four weeks' time.

FOOTBALL LEAGUE CUP FINAL

LIVERPOOL 1 BIRMINGHAM CITY 1
(5-4 on penalties)
25 February 2001

This was Liverpool's first appearance in the League Cup final for six years, while for Birmingham City it was their first since 1963. Liverpool had knocked out Chelsea (2-1), Stoke City (8-0 away, without the services of Stevie G), Fulham (3-0) and Crystal Palace (6-2 on aggregate) while Blues, who at the time were a second-tier team, based in Division One, had ousted Southend United (5-0 on aggregate), Wycombe Wanderers (5-3 over two legs), Tottenham Hotspur (3-1 at White Hart Lane), Newcastle United (2-1 at St Andrew's) and Ipswich Town (4-2 on aggregate in the semi-final).

Liverpool were red-hot favourites to lift the trophy at Cardiff's Millennium Stadium, but manager Gerard Houllier said in a pre-match interview: 'They [Birmingham] will be tough opponents. Trevor Francis has assembled a very good team, a group of players who will be relishing the challenge. Don't take anything for granted.' Steven Gerrard agreed with his manager, saying: 'I know Birmingham will be hard to break down. They defend in numbers and we will have to be on top of our game to beat them. It will be a difficult match, I'm sure of that.'

Liverpool (4-4-2): Westerveld, Babbel, Henchoz, Hyypiä, Carragher, Gerrard (McAllister), Hamann, Biscan (Ziege), Smicer (Barmby), Heskey, Fowler.
Birmingham City (4-4-2): Bennett, Eaden, Purse, Johnson, Grainger, McCarthy, Sonner (Hughes), O'Connor, Lazaridis, Horsfield (Marcelo), Adebola (Johnson).
Attendance: 73,500

After a hard fought and at times intriguing contest, it was Liverpool who emerged from the lottery of a penalty shoot-out to end six years without a trophy as they beat plucky Birmingham City 5-4 on spot kicks. It was Reds' goalkeeper Sander Westerveld who became Liverpool's hero when he saved two penalties, the first from full-back Martin Grainger and then what proved to be the decider, to deny substitute Andy Johnson. Blues boss Trevor Francis was in tears as he embraced youngster Johnson after he missed the crucial 12-yard-kick that left the gallant Midland underdogs in agony.

Liverpool were on course to lift the trophy after Robbie Fowler had scored a quite brilliant 29th minute goal, but battling Birmingham simply refused to lie down. Their noble efforts were rewarded when defender Stephane Henchoz fouled Martin O'Connor in the second minute of injury time, allowing centre-back Darren Purse to step up, showing remarkable courage and coolness, to level things up from the spot and take the game into extra-time. As then tension mounted, there were a handful of chances for both sides during the extra period before it was left for the lottery of a penalty shoot-out to decide the winners.

Blues, confident and comfortable on the ball, got better as the game progressed, but in the end Lady Luck smiled on Liverpool as they celebrated their first trophy success since 1995, when they beat Bolton Wanderers 2-1 to win the Coca-Cola League Cup at Wembley. Liverpool won the League Cup for the sixth time with successful penalties scored by Gary McAllister, Nick Barmby, Christian Ziege, Fowler and Jamie Carragher. Dietmar Hamann missed when it was 3-2 in Liverpool's favour. Birmingham scored through Purse, Marcelo, Aussie Stan Lazaridis and Bryan Hughes, after Grainger had missed their first kick. Dietmar Hamann missed for Liverpool, but Westerveld's saves from Grainger and Johnson tipped the balance back in favour of the Merseysiders.

Liverpool boss Houllier chose to shuffle his line-up, making four changes from the side which scraped into the UEFA Cup quarter-final after a rather controversial encounter with AS Roma.

Steven Gerrard was perhaps the surprise choice, named in the right-wing back position, despite being ruled out of the England squad with a groin injury. Blues who made a solid start, were almost undone in the 7th minute but Fowler, unmarked at the far post, failed to make a solid contact with Vladimir Smicer's cross. Birmingham, enjoying a lot of possession with Geoff Horsfield and Lazaridis their main threats, unfortunately failed to create a clear-cut chance as a result falling behind just before the half-hour mark. Stephane Henchoz's long clearance was knocked on by Emile Heskey for Fowler who, taking aim, found the net with a brilliant effort that flew over the head of Blues goalkeeper Ian Bennett from 25 yards out. Bennett was off his line, but all credit to Fowler for an instinctive strike that demonstrated his class. With Blues pushing forward, Liverpool's Czech star, Smicer, missed a sitter on the stroke of half time after Heskey had set him up.

Youngster Andy Johnson came on for Dele Adebola at the start of the second-half, equalising as he turned Nicky Eaden's cross inches wide of Westerveld's post. Liverpool replied immediately and a terrific saving tackle from Darren Purse blocked Fowler after a rare foray forward by Markus Babbel. Birmingham, full of energy, came again but it was Liverpool who came closest to adding to their score when Heskey, unmarked, blazed wildly over the top before Smicer was denied by Bennett after a smart flick by Fowler. Blues boss Francis then held his head in anguish on the touchline as Purse headed wide, totally unmarked following a corner.

Houllier made changes to protect Liverpool's lead, introducing Barmby and McAllister for the tiring Gerrard and Smicer. With time almost up, Blues were thrown a lifeline by referee David Elleray, who awarded them a penalty after Martyn O'Connor was flattened inside the area by a reckless Henchoz tackle. Purse, who had been limping heavily from cramp, showed tremendous courage to step forward after a lengthy delay to beat Westerveld.

It was a body blow for Liverpool and it gave Birmingham a massive boost and substitute Bryan Hughes – a boyhood Everton fan – almost scored his dream goal after 99 minutes with a brilliant chip from 30 yards that brought an outstanding save from Westerveld.

Liverpool then had an amazing escape when Johnson was clearly hauled down by Henchoz, but this time Elleray waved away the penalty appeals – the wrong decision. A header by Fowler forced Bennett into a brilliant save and the 'keeper then dived low to his right to clutch another header from Sami Hyypiä and as the tension mounted, rattled an upright from 30 yards.

Then came penalties – agony for Birmingham and ecstasy for Liverpool.

PREMIER LEAGUE

LIVERPOOL 2 MANCHESTER UNITED 0
31 March 2001

Prior to this long-awaited and much-anticipated annual home encounter with bitter rivals Manchester United, Liverpool had drawn at Sunderland, lost at Leicester and had been held at home by Derby County. Steven Gerrard, who came off the bench during the last game against the Rams, was back in the starting line-up for the clash with Alex Ferguson's Reds who, as League leaders, had lost only twice in the Premiership all season – once against Liverpool at Old Trafford in mid-December when Danny Murphy scored the 43rd minute winner.

Liverpool, and indeed Steven Gerrard, were up for this one alright and in front of the biggest Anfield crowd of the season at the time; they were confident of victory, which would of course clinch the double over the enemy.

Liverpool (4-4-2): Westerveld, Carragher, Hyypiä, Henchoz, Babbel, Hamann, Murphy, Gerrard (Owen), Berger (Barmby), Fowler (McAllister), Heskey.
Manchester United (4-4-2): Barthez, P. Neville, Brown, Irwin (Silvestre), G. Neville, Keane, Beckham, Butt (Scholes), Giggs, Sheringham (Chadwick), Yorke.
Attendance: 44,806

Referee Graham Poll (from Tring) got things moving and straightaway it was Liverpool who went on the offensive, with Robbie Fowler firing wide after just 2 minutes. United hit back and Dwight Yorke headed over before Phil Neville cleared his lines well, with Fowler closing in.

On 13 minutes Ryan Giggs saw his low shot well saved by Sandor Westerveld, but 3 minutes later, at the opposite end of the field, Liverpool took the lead. Fowler controlled the ball and laid it off to Steven Gerrard who, taking aim from fully 35 yards, beat Fabien Barthez with a cracking right-footed drive. A great goal.

Back came United, and Roy Keane had a shot parried before Emile Heskey fired a shot through Barthez's legs, only for the French goalkeeper to recover and dive on the ball inches before it crossed the line.

4 minutes before half-time, Liverpool scored again. Gerrard chipped the ball

forward to Fowler, took a required second touch and powered his shot past the stranded Barthez. Soon afterwards, Heskey had a chance to make it 3-0 but miscued his shot from 12 yards.

Early in the second half, Nicky Butt was off target from 20 yards as United pushed more men forward, and then David Beckham had an effort blocked while, at the other end, Danny Murphy shot wide following Gerrard's cushioned header.

In the 69th minute, soon after Dwight Yorke had a goal ruled out for offside, Liverpool were reduced to ten men when Murphy was shown a second yellow card for a robust challenge on full-back Denis Irwin. Gerard Houllier then brought on Gary McAllister and Nicky Barmby for Fowler and Patrick Berger, as United gambled by playing four up front. Liverpool's defence held firm, however, and on the break Heskey skimmed a low shot wide while Gerrard fired over.

United kept battling away and Yorke had a strong shot saved by the impressive Westerveld before the same player produced United's best effort of the half, but to no avail.

United ran out of steam, Liverpool held firm and duly completed a Premiership double over United. By doing so, they dramatically improved their chances of winning the Champions League.

PREMIER LEAGUE
EVERTON 2 LIVERPOOL 3
16 April 2001

Liverpool went in to this, the 164th Merseyside Derby, knowing they hadn't won at Goodison Park since 1990. Victory against their arch-rivals would clinch a place in the Champions League as well as earning them their first double over the Blues for over twenty years, having won 3-1 at Anfield earlier in the season when Everton had Thomas Gravesen sent off.

Covering the game for The Guardian *newspaper, reporter Paul Walker said: 'It may have been chaotic, its spiteful edge never blunted amid the flurry of yellow cards, but Liverpool emerged last night victorious ... just ... with Gary McAllister's dramatic stoppage-time winner, justifiable reward for a wonderful team performance'.*

Both Gary and Steven Gerrard had excellent games in midfield, while Emile Heskey was worth his weight in gold up front, and the final scoreline of 3-2 in Liverpool's favour indicated what a close encounter it was. It was a superb Merseyside Derby – one of the best for many a year – and if the truth be known, although Everton fought back to equalise twice, the Reds were worthy winners.

Everton (5-3-2): Gerrard, Abel Xavier, Ball, Gough (Alexandersson), Unsworth, Watson, (Pistone), Weir, Gemmill, Campbell, Ferguson, Nyarko.
Liverpool (4-4-2): Westerveld, Babbel, Carragher, Henchoz, Hyypiä, Biscan, Hamann, McAllister, Smicer, Fowler (Vignal), Heskey.
Attendance: 40,260

'We deserved to win', said Liverpool manager Gerard Houllier, despite his side losing Croatian Igor Biscan, who was shown two of the match's twelve yellow cards.

Liverpool stayed calm throughout the 90 minutes, even with ten men. They were strong and solid and well worth their victory. It was certainly a bit frantic during the last 10 minutes when Everton were put under pressure and the winning goal provided the sting in the tail of a rumbustious contest.

Unfortunately, before the start of the game, the Everton supporters made it a less than well-respected minute's silence in memory of the Hillsborough disaster. This set the tone, and as a result the hosts, who had six players booked, faced a £25,000 fine from the FA. Niggling free-kicks and snappy individual duals added to the flavour of a terrific contest, which saw the visitors take the lead before the whirlwind start had blown itself out.

Surprisingly, in the 4th minute a clear handball by Jamie Carragher was missed by referee Jeff Winter as he cleared his lines in a cluttered penalty area. The loose ball was sipped to Dietmar Hamann by Robbie Fowler and with Everton overcommitted, Emile Heskey controlled the German's astute pass, held off the retreating Steven Watson and thumped in his 21st goal of the season past 'keeper Paul Gerrard.

The action continued at breakneck pace and chances went begging at both ends of the field, mostly by poor defending rather than player creativity. The easiest fell to Everton, whose rusty striker Duncan Ferguson missed his kick in front of goal after a square pass from Scot Gemmill. After Sami Hyypiä's horrible clearance fell to Watson, Sander Westerveld flapped at the full-back's cross but Gemmill's improvised header thankfully drifted wide.

Liverpool had a couple of chances to extend their lead, but Fowler and Heskey failed to capitalise on openings and this encouraged Everton who equalised 3 minutes before the interval. Ferguson flicked Michael Ball's forward pass into the danger zone for Campbell to chase and, although Carragher managed to prod the ball away from the striker's feet, the 'Bluenose' favourite Scotsman, 'Big Dunk', followed up to smash in the equaliser, celebrating in style by taking his shirt off and swirling it above his head. The goal should have given the home side a half-time boost, but instead it was Liverpool who scored again in the 57th minute.

Between them, Liverpool's packed defence dealt with an Everton corner and Fowler, collecting Hamann's 60-yard pass, ran on unchecked into the area before attempting to find Vladimir Smicer. His pass, however, deflected off Ball and rolled behind two back-pedalling defenders and into the path of Markus Babbel who, taking aim, drove his low right-foot shot into the far corner of Gerrard's net. Within a minute, Liverpool should have gone 3-1 up. Scottish international Richard Gough was cruelly penalised as Fowler went down in the area. Loud booing greeted the striker, who stuttered in his run-up before cracking the spot kick, left-footed, against 'keeper Gerrard's left-hand post.

Then came Biscan's dismissal – Liverpool's third red card in four Premiership contests, which gave Everton impetus. With their fans behind them, they went for the jugular! Westerveld saved a point blank header from Abel Xavier as Everton powered forward and with the momentum clearly with the home side, in the 83rd minute, Hyypiä was penalised for holding down Ferguson and up stepped David Unsworth to bang home the equaliser from the spot. This set up a right royal, frenzied finish. With time virtually up, Everton's Alexanderson, tracking back, committed a foul some 40 yards out.

Everton pulled every player back. There seemed no way through but, with 'keeper Paul Gerrard expecting a lofted ball into the box, Gary McAllister chose to strike his dipping free-kick towards goal, and he succeeded by finding the bottom right-hand corner of Gerrard's net. It was a wonder goal which stunned the home crowd and set the travelling Red Army into raptures. As the players left the field, there were angry words between Everton's 'keeper Gerrard and his team-mate Michael Ball while the Liverpool players hugged each other as if they had won the Premiership title.

UEFA CUP SEMI-FINAL, 2ND LEG
LIVERPOOL 1 CF BARCELONA 0
(1-0 on aggregate)
19 April 2001

Liverpool, chasing their first European trophy in sixteen years, were confident of reaching the UEFA Cup at the expense of Spanish giants Barcelona, having battled hard and long to earn a goalless draw in what was a rather drab first-leg encounter in front of 90,832 fans at the Camp Nou a fortnight earlier.

Manager Gerard Houllier was able to field his strongest line-up, bringing back Steven Gerrard and Michael Owen. Before the match he urged the Anfield crowd to 'get behind the players from the word go.'

Liverpool (4-4-2): Westerveld, Babbel, Henchoz, Hyypiä, Carragher, Gerrard (Murphy), Hamann, McAllister, Smicer (Fowler), Heskey, Owen (Berger).
Barcelona (4-4-2): Reina, Reiziger (Simao), de Boer, Puyol, Luis Enrique, Petit, Cocu, Guardiola, Overmars (Garcia Lara), Rivaldo, Kluivert.
Attendance: 44,489

Swiss referee Urs Meier was in charge of what was one of Liverpool's most important cup matches for quite some time, and after early pressure he quickly awarded the Reds a free-kick from which Emile Heskey put nineteen-year-old goalkeeper Pepe Reina (later to move to Anfield) under pressure. But it was the visitors who had the first effort on target when a 35-yard rocket delivered by Brazilian striker Rivaldo was tipped over the bar by Sander Westerveld. In reply Owen found space but was denied when Reina produced a fine smothering save. Vladimir Smicer and Sami Hyypiä both put in weak headers and Steven Gerrard blasted a free-kick over as Liverpool responded.

The game was wide open and chances were being created as Emmanuel Petit, Marc Overmars, Patrick Kluivert (Barcelona) and Michael Owen all failed to get a decent contact on the ball when well placed. Almost immediately Luis Enrique shaved Westerveld's post, strongman Hyypiä put in a great tackle to deny the dangerous Kluivert as play intensified, and appeals for a penalty, as Gerrard went down inside the box, were waved aside by referee Meier.

A minute before half-time Liverpool did win a spot kick when Kluivert, helping out his defence, handled Gary McAllister's corner. The Scottish midfielder stepped up to thump the ball high into the net and give his side a vital half-time lead they just about deserved. This set up a mouth-watering second-half, with the onus clearly on Barcelona to attack – and they did just that, having come from behind to draw their previous two games.

Kluivert fired across the face of goal, with Luis Enrique unmarked 6 yards out and for five minutes Liverpool simply couldn't get out of their own half. Then out of the blue, Gerrard whipped over a teasing right-wing cross, but Heskey was thwarted by Michael Reiziger's timely challenge. A fumble by Westerveld almost let in Kluivert while at the other end of the pitch, Heskey's shot was saved by Reina while Gerrard's brilliant 40-yard drive flew just 6 inches wide.

The atmosphere was tense as Barcelona pushed forward, knowing that a goal would take them into the final, but Liverpool's held firm with Hyypiä and Stephane Henchoz quite outstanding. With time running out, McAllister and Dietmar Hamann both had long range shots at goal while substitute Robbie Fowler and Heskey put efforts over the bar. As the minutes ticked by – with 'You'll Never Walk Alone' ringing loudly round Anfield – Man of the Match Hyypiä repelled the danger with a terrific header as Kluivert and Carles Puyol challenged for a high ball. Soon afterwards the final whistle sounded amid joyous scenes at Anfield

Liverpool had made kit into their ninth European final after a dogged, resilient performance, thoroughly deserving their 1-0 aggregate victory which was built on towering defensive performance, epitomized by the efforts of Hyypiä and Henchoz.

With this clean-sheet, Liverpool had conceded just one goal in six Champions League games against AS Roma, FC Porto and Barcelona. The Reds will now face another Spanish club, Alaves, in the final in Dortmund on 16 May – just four days after taking on Arsenal in the FA Cup final.

FA CUP FINAL
ARSENAL 1 LIVERPOOL 2
12 May 2001

For Arsenal this was their fourteenth appearance in the final (seven wins, six defeats), while for Liverpool it was their twelfth (five wins and also six losses).

The Gunners, having scored fifteen goals in five ties to reach the final, including six away at London neighbours Queen's Park Rangers, were regarded as favourites by most bookies to beat Gerard Houllier's side, but with both managers able to field their strongest starting elevens, the neutral supporters were backing Liverpool who, of course, were going for a cup treble, having already lifted the League Cup and had the UEFA Cup final still to come.

Robbie Fowler was the victim of Houllier's decision to halt his attacking rotation policy, as he was left out of the starting line-up with Emile Heskey and Michael Owen up front. Arsenal boss Arsene Wenger resisted the temptation to recall Dennis Bergkamp after a lengthy absence through injury, pairing Thierry Henry and Sylvain Wiltord up front. Liverpool had lost two previous finals against Arsenal, 2-0 in 1950 and 2-1 in 1971.

Arsenal (4-4-2): Seaman, Dixon (Bergkamp), Keown, Adams, Cole, Pires, Grimandi, Vieira, Ljungberg (Kanu), Wiltord (Parlour), Henry.
Liverpool (4-4-2): Westerveld, Babbel, Henchoz, Hyypiä, Carragher, Murphy (Berger), Gerrard, Hamann (McAllister) Smicer (Fowler), Heskey, Owen.
Attendance: 72,377

In front of a capacity crowd at the Millennium Stadium in Cardiff – 35,000 supporting the team from Anfield – Liverpool from the outset looked intent on adopting a counter-attacking approach, allowing Arsenal space and possession until they reached the danger area. Indeed, the Gunners certainly dominated the opening exchanges, but gradually Liverpool came into the match.

Despite Arsenal seemingly in control, Emile Heskey was involved in the first contentious moment after just 6 minutes, when he tumbled under a challenge from Gilles Grimandi, but Bristol referee Steven Dunn correctly waved away Liverpool's appeals for a penalty.

10 minutes later, the Londoners had a much stronger claim for a spot kick. Fredrik Ljungberg released French striker Thierry Henry, who broke free of Liverpool's offside trap, skipped around goalkeeper Sander Westerveld and fired a shot which was, according to TV replays afterwards, certainly blocked on the line by the arm of Liverpool defender Stéphane Henchoz. The officials failed to spot the offence, despite Henry's confident appeals!

Despite a couple of half-chances for Liverpool – a Michael Owen shot that was closed down by Martin Keown, and a Steven Gerrard effort from long range that went well wide – there were no other major goalmouth incidents in a rather slow-moving and lacklustre first half.

As Arsenal started the first half well, it was Liverpool who shot out of the traps after half-time and, in the 47th minute, Gunners goalkeeper David Seaman was forced into action when he had to push the ball away to safety with his left hand after Heskey had powered in a header from Danny Murphy's free-kick.

Arsenal hit back and in the 56th minute dangerman Henry juggled the ball and switched passes with compatriot Robert Pirès, but was denied by Liverpool 'keeper Sandor Westerveld. Ashley Cole was first to the rebound and fired goalwards, but Liverpool captain Sami Hyypiä was in the right position to clear off the line. Defender Hyypiä rescued Liverpool again in the 67th minute, when he headed a Ljungberg lob off the line with Westerveld beaten.

With barely 20 minutes left, the deadlock was finally broken. Midfielder Patrick Vieira latched onto a poor clearance by Westerveld, feeding Pirès who smartly played Ljungberg clean through the middle of Liverpool's back four. The Swede ran on and duly rounded the Dutch goalkeeper, before firing home to send the Arsenal fans delirious! Moments later Henry had the chance to make it 2-0, but was denied by an excellent point-blank save by Westerveld.

Liverpool somehow survived the Arsenal onslaught, and after Houllier had introduced substitutes Patrik Berger and top-scorer Robbie Fowler for Danny Murphy, and the ineffective Vladimir Smicer in the 77th minute, the game changed dramatically.

Gerrard, who had been in a right old battle all afternoon with Patrick Vieira, started to find more space and, as a result, Liverpool at long last found a foothold in the game; after a series of raids into the Arsenal half, Michael Owen gleefully equalised with 8 minutes left. Arsenal failed to clear a free-kick delivered into the danger-zone by Gary McAllister who had replaced in the limping Dietmar Hamann on the hour. The lively Owen pounced with a right-foot finish, low past Seaman, from 8 yards.

Arsenal were suddenly on the rack as Liverpool drove forward confidently with Gerrard leading the way. In the 88th minute, with extra-time looming, the comeback was completed. Owen, looking lively and threatening, was released down the left by a wonderfully weighted long pass from Berger, and after controlling the ball he outpaced both fellow England teammates Tony Adams and Lee Dixon before belting in a right-foot shot hard and low across the diving Seaman into the far corner.

Arsenal, shell-shocked to say the least, threw the kitchen sink at the Liverpool defence but the 'red wall' held firm and so recorded victory, to the delight of their travelling supporters. This was certainly sweet revenge for those two previous defeats at Wembley.

11

UEFA CUP FINAL
LIVERPOOL 5 DEPORTIVO ALAVES 4
16 May 2001

Liverpool – fresh from their FA Cup triumph – had qualified for their first European final since the Heysel Stadium disaster encounter against Juventus in 1985, by knocking out (all on aggregate) Rapid Bucuresti (1-0), Slovan Liberec (4-2), Olympiacos (4-2), AS Roma (2-01), FC Porto (2-0) and, of course, Barcelona (1-0).

Gerard Houllier's men were strong favourites to beat the Spanish side Alaves, who didn't have a single domestic title to their name. Liverpool, on the other hand, had the largest trophy cabinet in English football. Together they were the perfect match – an odd couple in all fairness – but in truth Alaves were a much less well-renowned club, this being their first season ever in a major European competition.

They progressed to the final as one of the highest scoring teams in the competition, scoring at least four goals in each of their ties and putting five past mighty Inter Milan and nine past FC Kaiserslautern in the semi-finals across the two legs. This was Liverpool's third appearance in the UEFA Cup final appearance, their previous two in 1973 and 1976, had resulted in victories. Of course they were going for a cup treble in 2001.

'We will treat the game like every other. We start level and hopefully we can make our experience tell', said a confident Steven Gerrard.

Liverpool (4-4-2): Westerveld, Babbel, Henchoz (Smicer), Hyypiä, Carragher, Gerrard, Murphy, McAllister, Hamann, Heskey (Fowler), Owen (Berger).
Deportivo Alaves (3-5-1-1): Herrera, Karmona, Tellez, Eggen (Alonso), Contra, Geli, Cruyff, Tomic, Desio, Astudillo (Mocelin), Moreno (Pablo).
Attendance: 48,050

The atmosphere was electric inside the BVB Stadion in Dortmund when referee Gilles Veissiere from France set the ball rolling. Presenting a sharply contrasting challenge to Arsenal in the FA Cup final, Spanish giant-killers Alaves started brightly, but in the 4th minute Emile Heskey was fouled midway 35 yards from goal. Gary McAllister swung the free-kick into the middle of the penalty area towards Markus Babbel, who nipped between two rigid defenders to head the ball past Martin Herrera. What a start.

Experienced Alaves' coach Jose Manuel Esnal, known universally as Mane, chose to start with three at the back, hoping that a five-man midfield would restrict Liverpool's service to their front men. He was swiftly disillusioned as his side was simply torn to shreds by the speed and execution of Liverpool's movements.

In a rare attack, a 12th minute 30-yard free-kick thumped in by Oscar Tellez was dealt with by Liverpool 'keeper Sander Westerveld, but 4 minutes later Michael Owen, taking Dietmar Hamann's pass in his stride, turned provider by setting up Steven Gerrard for goal number two, the midfielder driving the ball hard and low into the Alaves net. Alaves' boss responded quickly by taking off defender Dan Eggen, who looked like a statue at the back, and bought on Ivan Alonso as an extra striker. It was the substitute who stunned Liverpool with a goal on 26 minutes, out-jumping Babbel at the far post to nod in Cosmin Contra's cross past Westerveld.

Liverpool, with Steven Gerrard having a tough time in centre-field with on loan Yugoslavian spoiler Ivan Tomic, were now on the back foot as they learned more of what Alaves were about. With Javi Moreno asserting himself up front, making life awkward for Stéphane Henchoz, the Spaniards poured forward in numbers, prepared to risk everything in an effort to grab the lead, but 5 minutes before the interval, they risked too much. Another excellent through ball from Hamann sent Owen clear. Goalkeeper Herrera raced out in an effort to avert the danger, but as Owen rounded him, the England striker was brought down. A stone wall penalty, and up stepped McAllister to calmly drive the spot kick past Herrera's left hand.

Alaves' boss, to his credit, quickly added another striker to his attack (Mango Mocelin), and all of a sudden Liverpool came under pressure. In the 51st minute, Javi Moreno – Spain's leading scorer – headed in his side's second goal from Cosmin Contra's superb cross from the left and 50 seconds later the same player brought the scores level at 3-3, smashing a free-kick low through Liverpool's defensive wall with an unsighted Westerveld having no idea where the ball was going until it passed him.

At this juncture, Houllier replaced the struggling Henchoz with Vladimir Smicer and withdrew Gerrard to shore up his defence on the right. But still Alaves threatened and, just past the hour mark, with the Liverpool fans roaring the side on, Heskey gave way to Fowler, while Pablo came on for Moreno who had taken a knock.

Fowler immediately found space to shoot at goal as the Alaves defence started to back-pedal and after two more half chances went begging Liverpool squeezed ahead once more with 17 minutes remaining. Collecting a pass from McAllister, Fowler brought the ball square before driving it full pelt inside Herrera's right-hand post. It was certainly tense stuff and with nothing to lose and everything to gain, Alaves simply went for broke and this absorbing encounter took another twist as Liverpool again wilted at a set-piece with just 2 minutes left on the watch. Jordi Cruyff, son of Johan, attacked an inswinging corner at the near post, connecting perfectly to send the tie into extra-time.

With the Golden Goal rule in force, the play during the early stages of extra time was predictably cagey, although Ivan Alonso thought he had scored for Alaves only to be given offside. And then, when Alaves' aggressive Mocelin was sent off in the 98th minute for a second bookable offence after fouling Babbel, it was advantage Liverpool. But could they make the extra man count?

Gerrard was off target with a long-range effort before a scintillating run and shot from Patrick Berger almost produced the winner. Then, it became nine against eleven when Alaves' defender Antonio Karmona was red-carded with just 4 minutes left of play. His dismissal for two yellows – the second for bringing down Vladimir Smicer – was crucial because from the resulting free-kick, taken by McAllister. Delfin Geli headed the ball into his own net to settle an absorbing encounter in Liverpool's favour after a titanic battle.

In the aftermath of the game, several pundits and journalists were claiming the final to be one of, if not the best ever in European competition. Former Liverpool defender Alan Hansen said it was 'The best final ever', and described Gary McAllister, who was directly involved in four of Liverpool's five goals, as 'The best player on the pitch'. At thirty-six, he was also the oldest and fully deserved his Man of the Match award. The hardworking Steven Gerrard also had a fine game ... so it was congratulations all round to Liverpool for achieving a hat-trick of cup final victories, going on to beat Charlton Athletic 4-0 in their last Premiership game of the season to pip Leeds United to third place and qualify for the Champions League for 2001/02.

Stevie G admitted that had never heard of Deportivo Alaves until two months before the final. He said: 'Over the last two months though, I took note. It's going to be a very hard game ... they would not have achieved what they have without a lot of hard work.' And so it proved, as Liverpool won their 25th cup game of the season to complete the treble.

12

CHAMPIONS LEAGUE, 3RD QUALIFYING ROUND
VALKEAKOSKEN HAKA 0 LIVERPOOL 5
8 August 2001

By virtue of finishing third in the Premiership in 2000/01, Liverpool qualified for the Champions League, but before embarking on a run with the 'big boys' of Europe they first had to get past FC Haka of Finland, who were not the greatest of opponents, and so it proved.

FC Haka (4-5-1): Vilnrotter, Karjalainen (Ivanov), Makela, Allto, Vaisanen, Popovits (Ruhanen), Torkelli (Pasanen), Kovacs, Wilson, Okkonen, Kangaskorpi.
Liverpool (4-4-2): Arphexad, Babbel, Henchoz, Hyypiä, Carragher, Berger, Hamann, Gerrard (Murphy), Litmanen (McAllister), Owen, Heskey (Fowler).
Attendance: 44,940

For this third qualifying round encounter, Gerard Houllier put out his strongest side in the Olympic Stadium in Valkeakoski near Helsinki, and after a slow start Liverpool completely dominated proceedings and took a giant step towards the group stages of the competition with a comfortable five-goal victory. Michael Owen stole the show, blasting home a second-half hat-trick to ensure the second leg at Anfield in a fortnight's time would be a formality. In all honesty, the first leg was something of a formality too. Totally one-sided, the final scoreline could easily have read 10-0, especially during the last half hour when the Finnish side tired considerably.

FC Haka, coached by Geordie Keith Armstrong, attempted to frustrate the visitors with a well-rehearsed offside trap and, for a while, the tactic worked. After a huge amount of Liverpool pressure, when Emile Heskey, Owen (twice) and Dietmar Hamann all went close, the deadlock was finally broken. The floodgates were opened by Heskey's close range header on 31 minutes.

Gerrard exposed a huge gap deep down the left-hand side of Haka's defence. He created enough space to deliver an inch-perfect cross into the danger zone towards the unmarked Heskey, who simply couldn't fail to miss. He didn't, moving in to crash a diving header beyond the reach of goalkeeper Andras Vilnrotter.

FC Haka, who were only awarded this third qualifying-round tie after Israeli outfit Maccabi Haifa were kicked out of the competition for fielding an ineligible player last week, were poor. The gulf in class between the Finns and Liverpool, the UEFA Cup holders was told, although all credit to the home supporters who were clearly intent on enjoying their night, no matter what the final result was. They cheered their team on non-stop, even when Liverpool were retaining possession, and that was continuously.

Liverpool and Finland captain Sami Hyypiä was cheered throughout the game by both sets of fans, as was fellow Finn Jari Litmanen, who was outstanding throughout, excelling in a deep lying forward role just behind strikers Heskey and Owen. The BBC reporter stated: 'Liverpool clearly relished the scenario in Finland's national stadium more than the prospect of a trip to the hostile home of Haifa and in the second half they really made themselves at home.'

Before the interval, Owen (twice more), Patrik Berger (with a pile-driver) and Litmanen could and should have increased Liverpool's lead, but it wasn't too long before the goals started to fly in. 11 minutes after half-time, Gerrard put in a fine tackle on the former Manchester United youngster David Wilson and quickly found Litmanen who, freeing himself from his marker, sprayed a magical pass forward to Owen who sprinted clear of the defence before picking his spot to double the lead. This was a clinical finish by the England star, who had missed a string of chances in the first half.

Litmanen's assist in the second goal was his last involvement in the game and he was duly substituted to a hero's reception, with Gary McAllister taking his place. After almost an hour's play, Liverpool became ruthless and completely took control of the match. In the 65th minute they scored a third goal when Owen nipped in for his second by rounding the stranded Vilnrotter to slot into an empty net, after Berger's clever chip over the home side's defence.

After dominating play for the next 20 minutes, during which time FC Haka hardly got a look in, there came the biggest cheer of the night when centre-back Hyypiä, up in attack, gleefully swept a loose ball home from 8 yards after Owen, with his hat-trick beckoning, had miskicked a McAllister cross. Owen's treble moment did arrive though just 90 seconds later, when he completed his hat-trick with a low drive from Berger's pass as a weary and deflated FC Haka defence merely looked on in admiration.

With time running out, and Liverpool toying with their opponents, Owen and substitute Robbie Fowler, with a clever chip after a 40-yard run, came close to adding to the goal county, while Berger, who along with Gerrard, had a terrific game in midfield, fired narrowly wide. Liverpool eased off in the return leg at Anfield and only scored four times, while FC Haka found the net once in reply.

Next up in Group B of the second qualifying stage, the Reds were to play three two-legged ties against Boavista, Borussia Dortmund and Dynamo Kiev.

13

European Super Cup
LIVERPOOL 3 BAYERN MUNICH 2
24 August 2001

Bayern Munich qualified for the Super Cup by winning the 2001 UEFA Champions League final, defeating Valencia 5-4 on penalties after the initial 1-1 draw. This was the German club's third appearance in the Super Cup, having previously competed in 1975 and 1976 against Dynamo Kiev and Anderlecht respectively, losing them both.

Liverpool qualified for the Super Cup as a result of winning the 2001 UEFA Cup with a 5-4 scoreline against a Spanish club. The Reds were appearing in their fourth Super Cup, having won the trophy in 1977 (v. Hamburg), but losing in 1978 to RSC Anderlecht and in 1984 to Juventus. For Steven Gerrard, this was, of course, his first Super Cup appearance ... and he was up for the challenge!

Liverpool (4-4-2): Westerveld, Babbel, Henchoz, Hyypiä, Carragher, Gerrard (Biscan), McAllister, Hamann, Riise (Murphy), Heskey, Owen (Fowler).
Bayern Munich (4-4-2): Kahn, Sagnol, Thiam, Robert Kovač, Linkle, Lizarazu, Sforza (Nico Kovač), Salihamidžić (Santa Cruz), Hargreaves, Elber, Pizarro (Jancker).
Attendance: 13,824

Bayern kicked off in the Stade Louis II Stadium in Monaco and threatened immediately, but it was Liverpool who created the first chance. Michael Owen crossed hard and low into the penalty area from the right, towards Emile Heskey, whose well-directed shot was deflected out for a corner. Bayern responded quickly, and midfielder Owen Hargreaves, later to join Manchester United and play for England, fired over the Liverpool bar.

In the 9th minute Liverpool were awarded a free-kick following a foul by Robert Kovač on Owen. This was taken by Gary McAllister and met by Markus Babbel, but the right-back's header went tamely over the top. With niggling fouls being committed all over the pitch – Gerrard being responsible for two clumsy ones – the first booking came in the 14th minute when Liverpool midfielder Dietmar Hamann was shown a yellow card after a mistimed tackle on Hasan Salihamidžić from behind.

At this stage in the proceedings, Bayern looked to be in control of the match but out of the blue, and completely against the run of play, Liverpool took the lead. Showing great determination, John Arne Riise, playing on the left side of midfield in front of Jamie Carragher, dispossessed Hargreaves. McAllister took control of the loose ball and passed to Gerrard, whose smart forward pass found Owen in ample space down the right side of the pitch. The striker whipped in a teasing low cross into the penalty area, which went beyond Heskey but found Riise who, following up the play, found the Bayern net with a well-placed shot. Bayern hit back hard and a deliberate foul by Gerrard on defensive midfielder Bixente Lizarazu resulted in a free-kick 25 yards from the goal. Thankfully, this came to nothing as Ciriaco Sforza's delivery was headed over the Liverpool goal by Pablo Thiam.

Liverpool regrouped and in their very next attack almost grabbed a second goal. Heskey's pass to Owen put him clear of the Bayern defence, but faced with a one-on-one situation with Oliver Kahn, the Liverpool front man attempted to chip the ball over the 'keeper, but failed to get the ball high enough. A second later Bayern went on the attack and their rugged defender Willy Sagnol held off Riise before crossing into the penalty area. The ball was met full on by Giovane Élber but his header went wide of the Liverpool goal.

With the first half drawing to an end Liverpool managed another attack, which resulted in a second goal. German Hamann, who was certainly enjoying the game against many of his fellow countrymen, slipped the ball to Heskey on the edge of the penalty area. He eased past his marker Thomas Linke and then took out Kovač, before shooting low beyond the stranded figure of Kahn.

Liverpool kicked-off the second half and within 13 seconds they had increased their lead to three. Carragher delivered a high ball into the Bayern half, defender Thiam missed his header, and as the ball dropped, Owen pounced, controlling it with his right foot before finding the net with his left. A fine goal. 12 minutes later Bayern reduced the deficit when Salihamidžić rose to head the ball firmly past 'keeper Sandor Westerveld from what was Bayern's first corner of the match.

Midway through the second period both teams made substitutions. Bayern took off Sforza, Claudio Pizarro and Salihamidžić and brought on Niko Kovač, Carsten Jancker and future Manchester City and Blackburn striker Roque Santa Cruz. Liverpool replaced Gerrard and Riise with Igor Biščan and Danny Murphy respectively. The game was hotting up, but Liverpool looked far more at ease than their opponents and cleverly passed the ball around in midfield. However, in the 82nd minute Bayern scored again to reduce Liverpool's advantage to just one and so set up what they thought would be a frantic finish! Substitute Jancker rose highest to head home a cross from Elber and immediately afterwards Bayern had a golden opportunity to equalise, but Lizarazu, free inside the area, shot straight at Westerveld.

No further clear-cut chances were created and at the end of the game it was Liverpool who celebrated with another famous victory over one of Europe's top sides.

This fine victory meant that Liverpool, and Gerrard of course, had won five trophies in five months, having already collected the FA Cup, the League Cup and UEFA Cup in 2000/01 and the FA Charity Shield just a few weeks previous.

Manager Gérard Houllier said: 'I must congratulate the players for what they've achieved. We know we are not perfect and we will continue to improve. But the team has shown they possess the winning edge, and this is what we have tried to develop.' Man of the Match against Bayern, Michael Owen, received a £10,000 cheque from the match sponsors, Carlsberg, which he presented to a charity of his choice.

14

INTERNATIONAL, WORLD CUP QUALIFIER
GERMANY 1 ENGLAND 5
1 September 2001

To soccer enthusiasts, the FIFA World Cup is the biggest show on earth, the holy grail for footballers from every corner of the globe. And over the years there have been some titanic battles involving top nations who go in search of glory in a competition that started back in 1930. Few rivalries, however, can match the history of England-Germany encounters. The first showdown had taken place way back in 1930 and ended in a 3-3 draw in Berlin. Up until this match in 2001 a further twenty-seven had taken place and England had won thirteen, including that memorable 4-2 victory in the 1966 World Cup final at Wembley.

The Germans gained some revenge for that defeat, notably at the 1970 and 1990 World Cups and also Euro '96 but also in the last meeting prior to this clash in Munich, they had defeated England 1-0 in a group qualifier which was, in fact, the last ever match staged at the old Wembley almost a year earlier, in October 2000. That result had ended the reign of manager and ex-Liverpool star Kevin Keegan, paving the way for the appointment of England's first foreign coach, Sven-Goran Eriksson. The Swede's side went into the return meeting in Munich trailing the Germans by six points, albeit with a game in hand.

The situation was simple – victory for Rudi Voller's side on home soil, where they were unbeaten since 1973, would secure a place at the Korea/Japan World Cup in 2002. A draw would leave the Germans requiring a point from their final game, meaning that England would have to compete in the play-offs. This was going to be one big game of football and Eriksson knew this, as did every Englishman in the world. He was able to field his strongest team against Germany who had suffered only one defeat in their previous sixty qualifying matches.

Germany (4-4-2): Kahn, Worns (Asamoah), Linke, Nowotny, Boehme, Hamann, Rehmer, Ballack (Klose), Deisler, Jancker, Neuville (Kehl).
England (4-4-2): Seaman, G. Neville, Ferdinand, Campbell, A. Cole, Barmby (McManaman), Scholes (Carragher), Gerrard (Hargreaves), Beckham, Heskey, Owen.
Attendance: 62,788

The stadium was buzzing in anticipation as the two teams took the field and it was Germany who started better than their old and bitter rivals, playing confident on-the-ground football. Yet there was no real hint at the drama that was to follow when Carsten Jancker prodded home the opening goal as early as the 5th minute.

Oliver Neuville headed down a lofted pass into England's penalty area, and with Rio Ferdinand and Sol Campbell both hesitating, Jancker was able to bundle the ball over the line, past goalkeeper David Seaman. However, while the Munich crowd sat back in anticipation of a memorable victory, Michael Owen had other ideas and 8 minutes later the ace marksman stunned Germany with a well-worked equaliser. The impish striker was fouled just outside the penalty area. Skipper David Beckham took the free-kick, which neither the attacking nor defending players managed to touch. However, overlapping right-back Gary Neville, lurking at the far side of the box, was able to head the ball back into the penalty area, where Nick Barmby nodded down to Owen, who netted with authority past the out of position Kahn. Thereafter, both a rejuvenated Seaman (with a majestic one-handed save from Jorg Boehme), and his opposite number Kahn, kept their goal intact, but chances were few and far between with each and every defender on the field putting in some terrific work.

2.5 minutes before the half-time whistle, England, by now fractionally ahead, were awarded another free-kick on the edge of the German 18-yard box, when the robust Jens Nowotny scythed down David Beckham on England's right flank. Beckham lined up the free-kick but failed to beat the German wall with his first attempt. But 'Golden Balls' quickly controlled Dietmar Hamann's clearing header and at the second attempt, delivered the perfect left-footed cross, deep into the penalty area. The ball found the head of Rio Ferdinand who nodded it back towards Steven Gerrard. His chest control was perfect, the finish sublime, as his unstoppable swerving shot flew hard and low into the bottom right-hand corner of Kahn's net from 25 yards out. The German 'keeper had no chance whatsoever of saving this epic strike.

It was a great goal – Stevie G's first for England – and it put his team in front and deservedly so. This was Gerrard's sixth senior outing for his country, having made his full international debut against Ukraine in May 2000 and England had won the previous five! 3 minutes into the second half, Beckham delivered a measured pass to Emile Heskey, who headed the ball down to an unmarked Owen who gleefully smashed it into the right-hand corner of the net. The diving Kahn managed to get a hand to the ball, but was unable to stop England taking a deserved 3-1 lead. The German supporters were shell-shocked as chants of 'England, England, England' rang round the stadium. All credit to the Germans though, who continued to attack and, indeed, they created a couple of chances, before England struck again in the 66th minute.

The outstanding Gerrard put in a crunching and successful tackle on Michael Ballack, which gave him possession in centre-field. Looking up, he delivered a great through ball for Owen, who sprinted into the box, looked up and fired over Kahn's head to give England a 4-1 lead. This was another wonderful strike that brought the Liverpool striker a deserved hat-trick – the first by an England player against Germany since Geoff Hurst's treble in the 1966 World Cup final.

England comfortably defended their big lead. Several German players looked down and out, although some did battle on despite the scoreline. In the 74th minute, England, playing keep ball, extended their lead to four with a thrusting attack. Centre-back Ferdinand won the ball and fed it to the feet of Manchester United's Paul Scholes. The midfielder made progress into the German half and after playing a smart one-two with Beckham, he found Heskey who ambled past a tired looking German defender, Marko Rehmer, before drilling his shot low wide of a depressed Kahn to make it 5-1.

The final quarter of an hour was relatively quiet. Germany were dead and buried and England, with no need to commit themselves, cruised home comfortably, referee Pierluigi Collina adding very little time on at the end, perhaps to save Germany from more embarrassment!

Some German fans left the game early in disgust, while the English fans celebrated their biggest victory since a 6-0 win over Luxembourg in 1999. It was England's biggest away win for eight years (they beat San Marino 7-1 in 1993) For Germany it was the first time they had conceded five goals since losing 6-3 to France in 1958, and only the third time in their history that they had lost by four goals or more. Germany would go on to concede another 5-1 defeat, against Romania in 2004.

Owen, Beckham, Gerrard and Ferdinand were outstanding in Munich. Elated and incredulous, the travelling England fans remained inside the stadium long after the final whistle to sing their heroes' praises and wave their Union Jacks, while back home a TV audience of nearly 15 million tuned in to watch history being made. Even the usually critical English press rushed to praise Eriksson's men, with the *Independent* reflecting on 'one of the least believable results in international sporting history' and the *Sunday Telegraph* left to wonder if it was all a 'magnificent, ridiculous dream'. Early the following year, a poll of Britain's 100 Greatest Sporting Moments ranked the win in Munich second, one place ahead of the 1966 final. The Germans, meanwhile, were stunned. Manager Voller slipped out of the stadium minutes after the final whistle to attend the bedside of his father, who had suffered a heart attack during the match, but legends such as Karl-Heinz Rummenigge were in no mood to show any mercy. 'I have never seen such a terrible defeat,' said the former star in the match's aftermath. 'This was a new Waterloo for us.'

A delighted Sven Goran Eriksson said: 'I can't believe that we can beat Germany 5-1 away. It seems like a dream, it's unbelievable. I said to the players: "I don't know what to say to you." I told them before the game, if you play football as you can play we can beat any team, even Germany away. But I can't believe it was 5-1.' German legend Franz Beckenbauer stated:

> I have never seen a better England team. They had pace, aggression, movement and skill. It was fantasy football. When they scored their third goal they started to play football that would have beaten anyone in the world. Steven Gerrard, Paul Scholes and David Beckham were brilliant in midfield and Michael Owen was simply unstoppable. Our defenders were slow and they just could not handle his pace, while his finishing was unbelievable.

England returned to match action four days after this epic win in Germany, with a 2-0 victory over Albania and when both sides drew their final group fixtures, Eriksson's side advanced automatically in the World Cup finals, thanks to their superior goal difference. As so often happens, however, the Germans enjoyed the last laugh, beating Ukraine in the play-offs and then, against all expectations, and odds, marched all the way to the final in the Far East, while England unfortunately made their customary quarter-final exit, going down 2-1 to Brazil.

15

PREMIER LEAGUE

LIVERPOOL 3 MANCHESTER UNITED 1
4 November 2001

Liverpool were going for a fourth straight win over their arch-rivals and there was no doubt that the entire team was 'ready for a battle'. Unbeaten in six Premiership games and in good form, the Reds were at full strength, Steven Gerrard having been declared fit to start after a slight knock.

Liverpool (4-4-2): Dudek, Carragher, Henchoz, Hyypiä, Riise, Murphy, Gerrard, Hamann, Smicer (Berger), Owen (Fowler), Heskey.
Manchester United (4-4-2): Barthez, G. Neville, Brown, Silvestre, Irwin (Yorke), Beckham (Scholes), Butt, Veron, Fortune, van Nistelrooy, Solskjaer.
Attendance: 44,361

Liverpool, it must be said, went out at Anfield and produced an impressive display to beat United in style, and realistically the scoreline could, and should, have been by a much wider margin. In-form striker Michael Owen scored twice either side of an unstoppable free-kick blasted home by left-back John Arne Riise. This defeat was United's second consecutive in the Premiership, following Bolton's surprise 2-1 win at Old Trafford a fortnight earlier.

Following Owen's first goal and Riise's bullet, David Beckham did pull a goal back as the visitors briefly threatened to make something of the match. But the Liverpool defence stood form and after Owen had netted for a second time, after a mistake by French goalkeeper Fabien Barthez, there was no way back for Alex Ferguson's men.

Liverpool, sitting on a six-match unbeaten Premiership run and lying fourth in the table, started like a team that clearly knew they had got the better of United on their previous three encounters.

The lively Owen gave an early sign of his intent by dragging the ball wide of the United goal after losing two defenders on the edge of the penalty area. Soon afterwards Emile Heskey fired wide and Steven Gerrard fired straight at Barthez. In fact, United struggled to get their game together during the opening half hour and Liverpool had two more chances to open their account before Owen finally found the net in the 32nd minute. It was a combination of United's frailties at the back and Owen's brilliance that produced Liverpool's first goal. Wes Brown failed to cut out Vladimir Smicer's through ball, to which Heskey got the faintest of flicks, allowing Owen a clear view of goal. The diminutive forward took control and with his right foot made no mistake, side-footing the ball deliberately and precisely into the top left-hand of Barthez's goal.

Although United picked up their game and actually enjoyed the greater possession for a short period of time, with Ruud van Nistelrooy threatening on a couple of occasions, it was Liverpool who struck again on 39 minutes to take a two-goal lead. Another needless foul by out-of-form Brown on Owen paved the way for Riise's thunderbolt free-kick, hammered home from almost 30 yards. Barthez never stood a chance and even if United had another goalkeeper on the line, he wouldn't have stopped the rocket anyway! Liverpool were in the ascendancy at this point and the impressive Gerrard came close to adding a third just before half-time.

As the players trooped off for a cuppa, those of Liverpool had their heads held high, having thoroughly deserved to take a 2-0 lead, whereas the eleven from United looked demoralized and totally disillusioned, knowing full well that home 'keeper Jerzy Dudek had not had one single save to make during the opening 45 minutes. United knew they needed to make an early breakthrough after the interval or the game was over, and they got one courtesy of their captain David Beckham.

Liverpool, on the back foot, failed to clear their lines and when the ball fell to Becks he smartly slipped home a left-foot shot wide of Dudek who had no hope of keeping the ball out. However, any thoughts United had of another Spurs-like comeback (they had been three down at White Hart Lane in late September before turning things round to win 5-3) were dashed 50 seconds later after a calamitous error by Barthez. The warning signs had been there for United in the opening minutes of the match, when Barthez failed to hold on to a cross which every other 'keeper would have collected without undue trouble, and he also fumbled two long-range efforts from Gerrard and Smicer and missed another high cross sent over by Danny Murphy. This time, the average French 'keeper was guilty of a similar mistake, allowing the unmarked Owen to head into an empty net with no one around him. Barthez simply stood still with his head in his hands. Liverpool could then afford the luxury of substituting two-goal hero Owen for Robbie Fowler and almost immediately the striker had a chance to make it four, while Gerrard – one of the best players on the pitch – speared another effort inches wide.

In a final attempt to give United's attack some potency Ferguson brought on Paul Scholes for Beckham, who seemed to be nursing a leg injury. The visitors pressed for a second, but could not find a way through a resolute Liverpool defence, which preserved their side's two-goal advantage to run out convincing winners.

After the game a stone-faced Ferguson confessed, 'We lost two terrible goals and that has been endemic throughout the season. Liverpool, who were by far the better side, thoroughly deserved their victory.' A delighted Steven Gerrard remarked, 'That was good, very good.' Commenting on Riise's goal, Michael Owen said, 'It was unbelievable. I've never seen a shot hit so hard and so accurately.'

16

PREMIER LEAGUE
LIVERPOOL 5 IPSWICH TOWN 0
11 May 2002

Ipswich Town simply had to win this game to stand any chance of avoiding relegation from the Premiership. In contrast, victory for Liverpool would mean they would claim the runner's-up spot behind Arsenal and so clinch an automatic place in the group stage of the 2002-03 Champion League. Second place would also be their highest finishing position since the Premiership started in 1992–93. This game also saw Gary McAllister make his farewell appearance for the Reds before leaving Anfield to take charge of Coventry City.

Liverpool (4-4-2): Dudek, Carragher, Henchoz, Hyypiä, Riise, Xavier (Anelka), Murphy (McAllister), Hamann, Gerrard (Smicer), Owen, Heskey.
Ipswich Town: Marshall, McGreal (Wilnis), Bramble, Hreidarsson, Venus, Clapham, Miller, Holland, Reuser, M. Bent (Armstrong), D. Bent (Stewart).
Attendance: 44,088

Liverpool had only lost one of their previous seventeen Premiership games, going down 1-0 at Tottenham a fortnight earlier; with two Michael Owen goals, they had walloped Ipswich 6-0 at Portman Road in early February and were in terrific form. Ipswich, in contrast, were struggling desperately, having won only one of their eleven matches since taking that battering from the Reds in front of their own fans. So let's be fair, the men team from East Anglia – who had won their previous two top flight games at Anfield – were never in with a chance once referee Steven Dunn set the ball rolling in front of a full house at Anfield.

It was vital for the Tractor Boys that they did not concede an early goal because they were certainly not going to score two themselves. Indeed, they had managed to find their opponent's net six times in their previous twelve Premiership matches.

Liverpool got going straightaway and after pinning the Ipswich defence back they struck in the 13th minute with a well-taken goal from overlapping left-back John Arne Riise. Ipswich 'keeper Andy Marshall struck his clearance against the back of midfielder Danny Murphy and with his teammates failing to spot the danger, Dietmar Hamann and Abel Xavier transferred the ball into the penalty area. The alert Owen dummied, allowing the incoming Riise to beat John McGreal to the ball before clinically firing home from 12 yards This effectively heralded the beginning of the end for George Burley's team ... or did it? To their credit, Ipswich refused to go down without a fight. Dutch international Martijn Reuser tested Jerzy Dudek with a long-range shot which the Liverpool 'keeper gathered without incident. Then, on 19 minutes, Jamie Clapham's right-wing cross was met at the far post by Darren Bent, whose effort was on bang on target until Dudek, stooping low, blocked the striker's header on the line.

Steven Gerrard, who had already made his mark with two fine tackles and a crisp shot that flew a yard or so wide, concerned manager Houllier (not to mention England boss Sven-Göran Eriksson) when he limped off in the 32nd minute to be replaced by Vladimir Smicer. The influential midfielder, who ironically had also left the field early in the first game at Portman Road, had raised his right hand moments earlier after striking a cross-field pass. The fact that he remained on the bench rather than going into the dressing-room for treatment clearly suggested he had a problem. Unfortunately, it proved to be a serious groin injury and as a result Stevie G failed to make the World Cup finals in South Korea and Japan.

With the fans roaring them on, Riise struck a magnificent second goal for Liverpool a minute after Gerrard had left the field. With his first major contribution, Smicer wriggled his way through the Ipswich defence, only to be brought down by John McGreal's clumsy challenge; but referee Dunn allowed play to continue, and when the ball broke free Riise was on hand to smash home a magnificent left-footer from just outside the area.

Things were not getting any easier for Ipswich. Reuser found himself free after beating Abel Xavier and Dudek, but saw his ferocious strike rebound harmlessly off an upright and things went from bad to worse after the break! The second half was only 42 seconds old when Town defender Titus Bramble twice attempted to steer the ball back to his goalkeeper. His second, a nervous back-header, was collected by Michael Owen who lobbed the ball over the stranded Andy Marshall and into an empty net. 3-0 ... game over ... Ipswich down!

11 minutes and three attacks later, Ipswich fell further behind. Smicer, unmarked, controlled the ball on the edge of the area and, evading two awkward-looking challenges from Hermann Hreidarsson and Mark Venus, he somehow managed drive the ball past Marshall. Emile Heskey might have added a spectacular fifth with a thumping volley from Owen's cross and substitute Gary McAllister almost brought the house down with another booming effort that just missed the target.

With time fast running out, it was left to French striker Nicolas Anelka, on loan from Paris Saint-Germain, to complete the formalities when he latched onto Owen's through-ball, ran clear of the defence and smartly beat Marshall from the edge of the 6-yard box for Liverpool's fifth.

17

WORTHINGTON LEAGUE CUP FINAL
LIVERPOOL 2 MANCHESTER UNITED 0
2 March 2003

En route to the final, Liverpool had knocked out Southampton 3-1, Ipswich Town 5-4 on penalties (after a 2-2 draw and the first time Steven Gerrard had skippered the team), Aston Villa 4-3 (away) and Sheffield United 3-2 on aggregate in the two-legged semi-final encounter.

United, meanwhile, had ousted Leicester City 2-0, Burnley 2-0, Chelsea 1-0 and Blackburn Rovers 4-2, over two legs in the semi-final.

Liverpool boss Gerard Houllier had a full squad to choose from, while his counterpart, Sir Alex Ferguson, was pleased to have Ryan Giggs, Paul Scholes and Wes Brown all fit to take their places.

Liverpool (4-4-2): Dudek, Carragher, Henchoz, Hyypiä, Riise, Diouf (Biscan), Hamann, Gerrard, Murphy, Owen, Heskey (Baros, then Smicer).
Manchester United (4-5-1): Barthez, G. Neville, Brown (Solskjaer), Ferdinand, Silvestre, Beckham, Keane, Veron, Scholes, Giggs, Van Nistelrooy.
Attendance: 74,390

Liverpool lifted the clouds from their troubled season by producing a gritty and determined display to win the League Cup for the seventh time. Star performer Steven Gerrard's first-half goal – a deflected shot off David Beckham – proved decisive in front of almost 74,500 spectators at the Millennium Stadium in Cardiff.

Michael Owen's breakaway 4 minutes from time put the icing on the cake and sealed a famous victory for Liverpool's much criticised manager Gerard Houllier. But on the day, it was Liverpool's goalkeeper Jerzy Dudek who was the star player. He was quite superb between the posts, keeping Sir Alex Ferguson's side at bay while his outfield players did the business elsewhere on the pitch. Dudek had been at fault earlier in the season when he presented Uruguayan striker Diego Forlan with a goal in United's Premiership win at Anfield, but he exorcised his demons in tremendous style, proving the cornerstone of Liverpool's win. The opening stages of this, the competition's 43rd final (the first was in 1961) were, in truth, action-free as both sides eyed each other up. It wasn't until the 21st minute that the first chance was created and it was United who almost broke the deadlock. Scholes released Giggs and his cross found Dutch striker Ruud van Nistelrooy, who flick drifted only inches wide of Dudek's far post.

During the last 20 minutes of the first half Liverpool began to take control and Owen, with a darting run, was thwarted by a sprawling block from French goalkeeper Fabien Barthez. 6 minutes before the interval, and perhaps against the run of play at that time, Liverpool edged in front with a goal which had a touch of good fortune attached to it.

The impressive and hard-working Gerrard, taking advantage of David Beckham's failure to close him down and collecting John Arne Riise's pass, powered in a wicked shot from 25 yards out. With Barthez right behind it, the ball suddenly took a wicked deflection off the England captain and looped over the United goalkeeper and into the unguarded net.

Liverpool had an astonishing escape on the stroke of half-time, when Dudek first blocked a well-struck shot from Juan Sebastian Veron. The rebound fell to the feet of Scholes, whose well-guided effort was turned over the top by the well-positioned Stephane Henchoz from virtually under the crossbar.

United, as they had to do, pushed more men forward from the start of the second half and Liverpool were grateful to Dudek's instinctive reaction save to deny van Nistelrooy on the hour mark. Meanwhile, Dorset referee Paul Durkin waved aside dubious penalty claims from both sides. At this juncture, Houllier was forced to make his first change, replacing the limping and hamstring victim Emile Heskey with Milan Baros. The tightly contested game was now beginning to open up a lot more and it was Barthez who kept United alive, saving a brilliant close-range effort from Gerrard after substitute Baros had broke clear on the counter-attack.

Suddenly the game was alive, the crowd was roaring, Gerrard was clapping his hands and urging on his players, but it was Dudek who was brought into action yet again when he denied the adventurous Scholes.

As United drove forward, Dudek once again saved superbly from van Nistelrooy, but with Liverpool living on a knife edge it was suddenly game over when Dietmar Hamann released Owen. The striker raced on, unchallenged, to beat Barthez with a clinical finish. This was a dogged contest, evenly balanced; but Liverpool had four players who produced something special when it mattered most – Dudek, Gerrard, Henchoz and ace marksman Owen.

A disappointed Sir Alex said after the game, 'The deciding factor was Liverpool's goalkeeper Jerzy Dudek – he was magnificent.'

18

PREMIER LEAGUE
WEST BROMWICH ALBION 0 LIVERPOOL 6
26 April 2003

Already relegated, Albion had won only two of their previous twenty Premiership games. They were also struggling to score goals – netting just twenty-six all season – while defensively they had kept only six clean-sheets. In contrast, Liverpool, with only two defeats suffered in thirteen games, were in good form. They had won the Merseyside derby just seven days earlier and were looking to complete the double over the Baggies, having won 2-0 at Anfield in September. Some bookmakers had as Liverpool 2:1 to win, while the odds for an Albion victory were as high as 10:1.

West Bromwich Albion (4-3-3): Hoult, Balis, Gregan (Jordao), Wallwork (J. Chambers), Clement, Johnson, McInnes, Koumas, Udeze (Lyttle), Dichio, Roberts.
Liverpool (4-4-2): Dudek, Carragher, Hyypiä, Traore, Riise (Diao), Diouf (Heskey), Murphy (Cheyrou), Hamann, Gerrard, Owen, Baros.
Attendance: 27,128.

Michael Owen – making his 185th appearance for the club – proved just how crucial he was to Liverpool's Champions League aspirations as he single-handedly demolished a poor West Brom side with four goals, taking his Premier League career tally to 102.

The England striker appeared subdued in the first half despite his 14th-minute goal separating the side at the interval, but after the break it was a completely different story as the Baggies simply collapsed. Owen doubled his and Liverpool's account almost immediately and within 22 minutes he had scored a second-half hat-trick. It also helped inflict upon Albion their worst home defeat for 125 years.

With Emile Heskey not 100 per cent fit following a back injury, Liverpool manager Gerard Houllier elected to start with Milan Baros alongside Owen up front. The Czech striker responded with two goals and could easily have had two more, but his efforts were totally overshadowed by the majestic finishing of Owen. With their reliable Icelandic defender Larus Sigurdsson missing, Albion's backline looked fragile from the start. As early as the sixth minute in, Danny Murphy's chip picked out Baros on the right but he scuffed his shot across the face of goal, just out of the reach of the onrushing Owen. 8 minutes later Murphy found Owen on the edge of the penalty area. The impish striker spun away from Baggies' captain Sean Gregan and drilled a precise, low shot past goalkeeper Russell Hoult's right hand, to open the scoring. Then, when Gregan fouled Owen 22 yards from goal, Murphy's free-kick was headed off the line by Derek McInnes. Baros then broke clear of the defence and looked certain to score, but just as he was about to pull the trigger, he slipped and the ball trickled out for a goal-kick.

Surprisingly, Liverpool were almost exposed in the 24th minute when Jason Roberts turned Djimi Traore, only for the defender to bring down the striker. Referee Dermot Gallagher waved a yellow card at Traore but Jason Koumas wasted the free-kick. Ronnie Wallwork then blazed over for Albion following a scramble in the box and only a last-ditch tackle by John Arne Riise prevented McInnes from equalising in the 39th minute. Soon afterwards, Danny Dichio's glancing header from Koumas' left-wing corner flew inches over Jerzy Dudek's crossbar.

The second half was only 3 minutes old when Liverpool went 2-0 up. Steven Gerrard's right-wing cross picked out Owen at the far post. His half-hit shot bounced into the path of Baros, who somehow diverted the ball into the net with the help of Gregan's leg. Seconds later it was 3-0. El Hadji Diouf crossed from the right. Baros and Owen both challenged for the ball and it was the latter who made contact, stabbing home his 100th Premier League goal. Owen was on fire, and in the 61st minute he completed his hat-trick. Baros raced clear of Clement down the right wing and from his low cross low the unmarked Owen side-footed in what would be the easiest goal of the afternoon.

Totally shell-shocked, Albion did enjoy a period of possession midway through the half but that fizzled away and in the 67th minute, Gerrard and Murphy set up Owen who slotted home his fourth goal to bring up Liverpool's nap-hand. Houllier quickly introduced Heskey for Diouf and straightaway Baros should have made it 6-0, but fired straight at the 'keeper. Dudek made his first real save in the 80th minute, tipping over a 25-yard drive from Albion's best player, Koumas. From Gerrard's excellent pass, Owen should have had his fifth as Liverpool responded, and when the influential midfielder played in Baros, Hoult was left stranded as the sixth goal flew in. The final act of a rather one-sided game saw Sami Hyypiä clear a Roberts shot off the line.

19

CHAMPIONS LEAGUE
LIVERPOOL 3 OLYMPIAKOS 1
8 December 2004

Having already played five of their Champions League Group A games – two of which had ended in 1-0 defeats against Olympiakos and AS Monaco – Liverpool knew they had to win their return fixture against the Greeks side to make it through to the knockout stage with Monaco. A draw would be no good whatsoever! This was to be one of the biggest games at Anfield for years.

Olympiakos were in good form, defensively sound, with three wins and a draw under their belts. They had defeated Monaco and La Coruna both by 1-0 and had conceded only two goals. Liverpool, languishing in seventh place in the Premiership, having drawn their last game 1-1 with Aston Villa, had not been playing well. Steven Gerrard was not, in his own words 'one hundred per-cent fit', having missed seven Premier League games already. But a Champions League game at Anfield invariably brings the best out of the Reds and everyone was up for a fight on the night…

Liverpool (4-4-2): Kirkland, Finnan (Josemi), Carragher, Hyypiä, Traore (Pongolle), Nunez, Alonso, Gerrard, Riise, Kewell, Baros (Mellor).
Olympiakos (4-4-2): Nikopolidis, Pantos, Anatolakis, Schurrer, Venetidis (Maric), Georgiadis (Rezic), Kafes, Stoltidis, Djordjevic, Rivaldo, Giovanni (Okkas).
Attendance: 42,045

The game itself was tense throughout but what a finish we had! Many fans looking downhearted were making their way to the exit doors, others were seated, biting their finger nails, but thousands were still roaring Liverpool on, to victory, they hoped. With time fast running out, up stepped Steven Gerrard to score a magnificent goal to clinch victory and send Liverpool into the knockout stages of the competition. Olympiakos had taken the lead through Brazilian Rivaldo, who netted from a free-kick after he had been brought down just outside the penalty area.

This left Liverpool needing to score three goals to go through. Mission impossible? Not at all. With the Anfield crowd behind, Rafael Benítez's men drove forward, pegging the Greek side back in their own half. It was hotting up, and when Florent Sinama Pongolle converted Harry Kewell's cross to equalise, the roof at the Kop end of the ground almost came off. When substitute Neil Mellor stabbed Liverpool in front from 6 yards, all hell broke loose. It was brilliant stuff, but another goal was still required. It was 'man of the moment' Mellor who teed up Gerrard to lash the ball home from 25 yards and win the match in style.

Liverpool came flying out of the blocks and won three corners in the first 2 minutes, one of which saw Milan Baros have a goal disallowed after Giorgos Anatolakis had been barged out of the way. Soon after, another dangerous Gerrard corner landed on Sami Hyypiä's head, but the Finn was disappointed when his effort went wide from 6 yards. Unfortunately Liverpool's bright and breezy start fizzled out as the Greeks gradually got going, retaining possession to frustrate the Anfield crowd, Rivaldo and Predrag Djordjevic being the two most influential players. A Rivaldo free-kick flicked off Gerrard's head and flew over 'keeper Chris Kirkland's crossbar before Liverpool replied with Baros flicking a left-wing cross onto Nikopolidis' post.

Rivaldo, in superb form, was stretching the home defence and in the 27th minute he created a goal with some brilliant play to knock the stuffing out of Rafael Benítez's side. The Brazilian skipped past four players before Hyypiä brought him down 20 yards out. Unmoved, Rivaldo picked himself up, placed the ball in position and curled the free-kick into the net – although Kirkland wasn't too happy when the 'Red' wall split in front of him! Another Rivaldo run was halted by a foul tackle from Jamie Carragher, who was booked. Then, the impressive Djordjevic smacked a free-kick into Kirkland's arms before Gerrard, who had already clipped an improvised effort against a post, got the Liverpool engine running on full throttle.

At the start of the second half, Benítez brought on Pongolle for Djimi Traore and the substitution immediately paid dividends, as the young French striker, arriving at the near post, put away Harry Kewell's cross to give the hosts renewed hope. The Greeks refused to buckle, though, and the game became heated with several off-the-ball clashes. Hyypiä and Carragher were both spoken to by Spanish referee Manuel Enrique Mejuto Gonzalez, who then yellow-carded Gerrard for a wild kick, which could well have resulted in a red! But Liverpool's captain was here, there and everywhere, desperately trying to haul his side back into it. He was desperately unlucky when his blistering 25-yard volley was ruled out because Baros had fouled Gabriel Schurrer. Sadly, for Gerrard, his teammates were not up to the same standard. Kewell headed straight at Nikopolidis from 5 yards when it looked easier to score, Baros failed to make contact when well placed and Alonso was way off target with a speculative long-range effort.

Having seen Pongolle make a huge impact, Benítez tried his luck with Ian Mellor, introducing the young striker in place of Baros in the 78th minute. And bingo, it happened again, as 3 minutes later Mellor was in the right spot at the right time to ram home Liverpool's second goal and set up a grandstand finish.

One more goal was required. The crowd turned the sound volume up to its limit and after Mellor and Pongolle both had penalty appeals turned down, it was left to Gerrard to whip in the all-important third goal with just 3.5 minutes remaining. Mellor did the spadework by setting Gerrard 8 yards or so outside the area. Pulling back his right foot, the midfielder released a bullet, which flew past Nikopolidis and into the net to send the crowd into raptures.

Perhaps Liverpool were fortunate to win 3-1, but for Gerrard it was nothing less than he deserved. He was quite magnificent, better than Rivaldo!

After the game, Stevie G admitted that at half-time it was looking hopeless. 'We thought we were out. We sat in the dressing room and everyone was gutted because we really thought that was it. No one said anything; we were just staring at the floor.' But the game was magically transformed by that wonderful Spaniard 'Rafa the gaffa'.

20

LEAGUE CUP FINAL
CHELSEA 3 LIVERPOOL 2
(After Extra Time)
27 February 2005

Liverpool's road to the final began with a 3-0 victory over Millwall when Salif Diao scoffed a 'rare' goal. Neil Mellor's brace against Middlesbrough in the next sealed a 2-0 victory before the Reds won a penalty shoot-out with Tottenham Hotspur in the quarter finals (after a 1-1 draw). Liverpool, in fact, had fallen behind to a Jermain Defoe goal in the 108th minute, before French U21 international Florent Sinama-Pongolle struck in a 117th minute penalty to take the game to a shoot-out, which Liverpool won 4-3. In the semi-final, Steven Gerrard netted the only goal in each leg as Liverpool beat plucky Watford 2-0 on aggregate.

Chelsea's passage to the final included victories over London neighbours West Ham United, Fulham, along with Newcastle and Manchester United.

This was Liverpool's 10th appearance in the League Cup final. It was also Rafael Benítez's first major final, as well as of his counterpart José Mourinho's first tenure at Chelsea.

Chelsea (4-5-1): Čech, P. Ferriera, Terry, Carvalho, Gallas (Kezman), Makelele, Jarosik (Gudjohnsen), Lampard, J. Cole (Johnson), Duff, Drogba.
Liverpool (4-4-2): Dudek, Finnan, Hyypiä, Carragher, Traore (Biscan), Hamann, Gerrard, Luis Garcia, Riise, Kewell (Nunez), Morientes (Baros).
Attendance: 77,902

Liverpool started the game supremely well with John Arne Riise crashing home a terrific volley after just 45 seconds – one the fastest goals ever scored in a domestic final. However, Chelsea exerted growing pressure as the game progressed and deservedly claimed an equaliser when the unfortunate Steven Gerrard conceded an own goal. There were chances at both ends of the field before the game went into extra time. It was Chelsea who proved the stronger, scoring twice through Didier Drogba and Mateja Kezman before Antonio Nunez pulled one back to set up a grandstand finish. In fact, spectators were still taking their seats when Riise, playing on the left side of midfield, found the net.

Fernando Morientes, participating in his 17th cup final of his career, collected an inch-perfect pass from Steven Gerrard, turned away from Claude Makélélé on the right and hit a lethal cross towards the far post. The Chelsea defence, including right-back Paulo Ferreira, had bunched in the middle of the penalty area and the ball eluded them all, allowing Riise, unmarked and totally free, to smash a volley beyond Petr Čech from the corner of the 6-yard box.

Unfortunately for Liverpool, by scoring so early, it allowed Chelsea plenty of time to collect themselves and José Mourinho's side could even afford to spend half an hour in shock before getting down to business and trying to beat the Reds! However, despite being a goal down, it must be said that from the 31st minute onwards Chelsea were far superior. They retained possession with a confidence that made it even more embarrassing for the travelling Liverpool supporters in a packed Millennium Stadium. It was annoying to see their favourites give the ball away so casually and with such carelessness – Gerrard included!

Liverpool did have a few fleeting moments for sure, but they never looked capable of beating in-form Čech in the Chelsea goal. He was superb, denying five players with consummate ease. In fact, Čech would not have played in the final had Carlo Cudicini, the back-up goalkeeper, not been suspended. At the other end of the field, Liverpool 'keeper Jerzy Dudek was also in good form and pulled off two excellent saves as Chelsea searched for an equaliser. Frank Lampard, who had been going through a muted spell, was an incessant danger with his range of passing, and he also had an effort blocked by Sami Hyypiä in front of goal with Dudek out of position.

Chances were created and missed; defenders of both teams, at times, looked rather uncertain, especially when high crosses were delivered into the danger zone. Both goals survived and Chelsea's Ivorian striker Drogba had the best chance, although his weak shot was easily turned aside by Dudek.

After early second-half pressure by Chelsea, which saw Steven Finnan foil Drogba with an excellent and unexpected challenge, Liverpool's German midfielder Didier Hamann worked a move with Luis Garcia on 64 minutes, but his shot from the edge of the area was saved at full length by Čech – a crucial save. With time fast running out and chances few and far between, Chelsea, completely against the run of play, found themselves level on 79 minutes when the unfortunate Gerrard conceded an own-goal.

Hamann was penalised on the right. Paulo Ferreira whipped over the free-kick into a packed penalty area. Gerrard, leaping in the midst of a group of teammates, got only a glancing touch on the ball with his head but it was strong enough to see it fly into his own net via the inside of the post. There is no doubt that the Liverpool skipper, who has so often willed his team to a win, had doomed his club here. 4 minutes earlier, he had spurned a great chance to guarantee victory when, from 6 yards, he drove a left-footer wide after a splendid cross from the substitute Antonio Nunez. That shock equaliser scrambled Chelsea's form for a while and Makélélé, who had been toiling through an error-ridden patch, suddenly found his form.

Liverpool were struggling to get their game back on track and Lampard's prompting, coupled with the darting runs of Damien Duff and the threat of Drogba through the middle, gave Chelsea the initiative. Riise headed a swerving cross by William Gallas over his own bar and soon afterwards Dudek, who hurt a knee in a double save from Duff, saved well from the impressive and dangerous Drogba. The Polish goalkeeper also parried a header from Eidur Gudjohnsen who had come on for Kezman, also thwarting Gallas from the rebound.

Mourinho immediately introduced Glen Johnson (later to join the Reds) as he reverted to choosing a sedate back four to protect Chelsea's interests. He knew, with Liverpool disconsolate and tiring, that he needed only to wait for victory as the game went into extra time. Right from the start of the first period of extra time Chelsea hit the accelerator pedal hard and after a series of threatening attacks, they edged in front in the 107th minute.

Johnson hurled a long throw deep into the Liverpool box from the right. The ball cleared Hyypiä at the near post and fell to Drogba who, anticipating a mistake by the Liverpool centre-back, pounced to slip the ball home from close range. 5 minutes later, Dudek failed to clear a teasing cross and was left completely stranded as Gudjohnsen turned the ball back for Kezman to knock in his fourth goal of the season and give Chelsea a huge advantage at 3-1.

Liverpool, urged on by Gerrard, responded as expected and the lively Nunez headed a scrappy second goal from Riise's throw-in with 7 minutes remaining. But Chelsea – compact in defence and midfield – were never going to let their lead slip and they held on comfortably to earn Mourinho his first trophy in English football, although the 'Special One' was not allowed on to the pitch at the end after being sent off, apparently for putting his finger to his lips to hush the Liverpool fans!

After the game, a disillusioned Gerrard said, 'We are obviously gutted. We played reasonably well but I will admit they were better than us on the day.' No less than fifteen overseas players started the final (seven from Chelsea) and five more entered the game as substitutes, the game itself starting an intense rivalry that developed between the two sides during Benítez's time in charge at Anfield.

21

CHAMPIONS LEAGUE FINAL
AC MILAN 3 LIVERPOOL 3
(LIVERPOOL 3-2 ON PENALTIES)
25 May 2005

After some exciting matches at home and away, en route to their sixth European Cup/Champions League final, Liverpool were regarded as underdogs against Serie A runners-up AC Milan.

The Reds had played no less than fourteen matches in the competition before making their way to Istanbul. They had won eight (beating both Chelsea and Juventus), drawn three (all 0-0) and lost three (each by a single goal). Defensively Liverpool had been reasonably sound, conceding only seven goals but AC Milan had scored seventeen times, including three successive threes.

Manager Rafael Benítez was, however, quietly confident that his players would perform on the night. And they did, but not until they had recovered from a disastrous first 45 minutes! After a stern half-time talk between manager, coaches and players alike, Liverpool came out fighting for the second half, and what an astonishing comeback they made – the best in the 50-year history of these 'European' finals. As a result the game went into extra time and then a dreaded penalty shoot-out, before the Reds claimed a memorable victory.

AC Milan (4-3-3): Dida, Cafu, Nesta, Stam, Maldini, Pirlo, Gattuso (Rui Costa), Kaká, Seedorf (Serginho), Crespo (Tomasson), Shevchenko.
Liverpool (4-4-2): Dudek, Finnan (Hamann), Carragher, Hyypiä, Traore, Xabi Alonso, Luis Garcia, Gerrard, Riise, Kewell (Smicer), Baros (Cisse).
Attendance: 64,869

Inside a packed Ataturk Olimpiyat Stadium in Turkey, and just 52 seconds after Spanish referee Manuel Garcia had blew the start whistle to get the fiftieth European Cup final underway and even before some spectators had sat down comfortably, Paolo Maldini fired Milan in front with the fastest-ever goal in the competition's history. The veteran left-back and captain of four winners' medals connected with the ball in a stunning right-footed volley from Andrea Pirlo's precise free-kick, sending the ball fizzing past Liverpool's Polish goalkeeper Jerzy Dudek like a rocket. Kaká had won the free-kick, drawing a foul by Djimi Traoré, but the goal failed to settle Milan's nerves completely.

After the hard-tackling midfielder Gennaro Gattuso had struck a free-kick from straight into touch, Liverpool's captain Steven Gerrard created chances for John Arne Riise and Sami Hyypiä, but neither troubled Milan's goalkeeper Nelson de Jesus Silva, (better known as Dida). Striker Hernán Crespo, on loan from Chelsea, and preferred in attack to Filippo Inzaghi and Jon Dahl Tomasson, almost scored a second for Milan with a near-post header following a 14th minute corner, but a combination of post and Luis García on the line prevented the ball from crossing the line.

Liverpool's cause was hardly helped when Aussie Harry Kewell, a surprise selection to partner Milan Baroš in attack, pulled up and had to be replaced by Vladimir Šmicer after just 23 minutes. At this juncture, Milan were playing with assurance and Liverpool were struggling. Pirlo was pulling the strings in midfield, Ricardo Kaká was running strongly through the middle and down both flanks and Crespo had to be marked closely. Unfortunately, he wasn't! Soon after Liverpool had enjoyed their brightest spell of the opening half, 6 minutes before the break they were caught on the counter-attack. Luis García had claims for a penalty against Alessandro Nesta ignored, and before you could blink an eye Milan surged upfield. The impressive Kaká found Ukrainian Andriy Shevchenko, who would move to Stamford Bridge in 2006, sprinting through the inside-right channel. He switched a square pass onto Crespo who drove the ball past Dudek.

The influential Kaká then produced a moment of shear magic to seemingly finish off Liverpool, or so it looked! Just before half-time the Brazilian swivelled away from his marker, checked and threaded a perfect pass through for Crespo, who went on to become only the third player to score twice in a Champions League final, netting low past a stranded Dudek.

Three goals down at half-time, Liverpool were shell-shocked, stunned and their hordes of travelling fans (35,000 of them) couldn't believe what had gone wrong. Manager Benítez brought on German Dietmar Hamann for Steven Finnan at the start of the second half. It was a masterstroke, and amazingly Liverpool, looking a totally different team, did not have long to wait to open their account.

After a powerful free-kick from Shevchenko was spectacularly tipped away to safety by Dudek, Gerrard rose to head imperiously past Dida from Riise's left-wing cross on 54 minutes. No one was going to stop Stevie G from finding the net on this occasion! Just 2 minutes later Šmicer, who was playing his last game for the club, finished off a move involving Alonso and Hamann with a well-struck right-footed shot that Milan's 'keeper could only help into the far corner of the net.

Liverpool were now on a roll. Milan didn't know what had hit them; the Italians were in a spin and definitely on the back foot! A swarm of red-shirted players powered forward and it came as no surprise when they were awarded a penalty on the hour mark following a foul by Gattuso on the impressive and hardworking Gerrard. Xabi Alonso took the spot kick, which was saved by Dida, but the Spaniard reacted quickest to score a deserved equaliser.

Liverpool were now dictating the game, their fans were delirious, there was a cacophony of sound inside the stadium and it was a terrific atmosphere. A fifth

European title and Liverpool's first for twenty-one years was there for the taking. Could they do it? However, after such a brilliant spell of attacking football, it was almost inevitable that Liverpool would tire, and they did, to a certain extent. But everyone was still focused on the game and left-back Traoré had to clear off the line from Shevchenko, before Jamie Carragher's last-ditch tackle foiled Kaká. Liverpool responded and Gerrard, finding space, held his hands high as his well-struck shot flew over the bar, suggesting that Milan were still vulnerable.

Late substitutions saw Djibril Cissé come on for Baroš, and Tomasson and Paulo Sergio Oliviera de Silva (known as Serginho) replaced Crespo and Dutchman Clarence Seedorf, but with time running out, no one really wanted to attack in numbers. These fresh legs were, of course, brought on for the additional 30 minutes and it was the Milan duo came who almost conjured up a goal in the first period of extra time, but Tomasson just failed to connect with Serginho's teasing cross.

Liverpool, with Gerrard now lying very deep, were content to punt long passes up to Cissé, but unfortunately he failed to make much headway, whereas Milan continued to look the more likely scorers in the second period. Indeed, they almost snatched victory with barely 2 minutes left, but Dudek produced a quite stunning double save to thwart Shevchenko from point-blank range and take the final to penalties. It proved to be a rather tense and nervous shoot-out. Milan went first; Serginho missed, firing over the bar; Hamann nervously scored for Liverpool (1-0); Pirlo's kick was saved by Dudek (still 1-0); Cisse tentatively scored for Liverpool (2-0); Tomasson scored for Milan (2-1); Riise's penalty was blocked by Dida (still 2-1); Kaka scored for Milan (2-2); Smicer scored for Liverpool (3-2).

Shevchenko, who had scored the winner in Milan's final shoot-out win with Juventus in the 2003 final, missed this time, seeing his effort saved by the Polish goalkeeper. Bingo, 3-2 to Liverpool. Dudek is the hero on the night and Liverpool arose as the new Champions of Europe.

Therefore, after a fantastic nail-biting contest, Liverpool joined Real Madrid, AC Milan themselves, Bayern Munich and Ajax Amsterdam in being awarded the famous and coveted European Champions trophy to keep.

After the game, a knackered Steven Gerrard admitted that 'Liverpool played for penalties. But weren't we great? All credit to the lads who battled every inch of the way and what a goalkeeper we have here.' It is not often that a cup final is accredited to one single player. This one was and Steven Gerrard was the star of the show in Turkey by a mile.

An estimated 900,000 fans, supporters, spectators, enthusiasts, call them what you like, crammed into the streets of Liverpool to welcome back their all-conquering heroes. As the open-top bus made its way round Anfield and through the city centre, Stevie G was heard to say: 'This is unbelievable.' Afterwards the skipper was overcome with emotion as he eased out these words: 'The welcome we received back home capped the greatest night of my life.' There is no doubt that this Istanbul final made Steven Gerrard a Liverpool legend.

22

FA CUP 6TH ROUND
BIRMINGHAM CITY 0 LIVERPOOL 7
21 March 2006

When this cup tie was played, Birmingham City were lying 18th in the Premiership while Liverpool were sitting as high as third and they had been beaten only once in their previous seven league games. Earlier in the season the Reds had drawn 2-2 at St Andrew's and were then held 1-1 at Anfield in Premiership matches. One of the biggest crowds of the season was expected at St Andrew's to see the battle of the colours: the Blues v. the Reds.

Birmingham City (4-4-2): Maik Taylor, Melchiot, Martin Taylor (Tebily), Cunningham Clapham, Clemence, Pennant, Johnson (Bruce), Forssell (Dunn), Painter.
Liverpool (4-5-1): Reina, Finnan, Carragher, Hyypiä, Traore (Kewell), Alonso, Luis Garcia, Sissoko, Gerrard (Cisse), Riise, Crouch (Morinentes).
Attendance: 27,378

'Birmingham bewitched, bothered and bewildered as Liverpool run riot' was the headline in *The Guardian* after the Reds blitzed the Blues in emphatic style.

Rafael Benítez's side, rampant throughout, cut through the home side effortlessly. To be blunt this non-event of a cup tie was nothing short of shooting practice for Liverpool, who eased into their 22nd FA Cup semi-final and their first for five years.

Having already scored eight goals in their previous three cup matches, and eight in four days in Premiership victories over Fulham and Newcastle, Liverpool were in excellent form, while Blues had only won one of their previous seven league matches. This was match No. 53 of the season for Liverpool and their second in just 72 hours, but they simply made mincemeat of their West Midland opponents and if they had stepped out of second gear, the final scoreline may well have been in double figures.

Blues fans were still taking their seats when Sami Hyypiä, who had been given the freedom of the Birmingham penalty area, headed past a startled Maik Taylor after just 54 seconds. Mohamed Sissoko, Liverpool's Mali international who started the game with protective goggles after suffering retina damage in Lisbon a month earlier, justified his place in the side by flicking on Steven Gerrard's free-kick for Hyypiä to nod in. It transpired that it wasn't the first time this season that home manager Steven Bruce had placed his head in his hands so early in a game – the marking was atrocious! Sissoko, who had not been a first choice in the Liverpool side, was also involved in the second goal. He fed Gerrard on the right and when the Reds' captain swept a fine ball into the area, the lanky figure of Peter Crouch, darting ahead of Kenny Cunningham, headed powerfully towards goal. Keeper Taylor was well placed to save but made a hash of his attempts to keep the ball out. Boos were now echoing around St Andrew's as Crouch turned away to celebrate his 11th goal of the season.

Liverpool, 2-0 up, hadn't even broken into a sweat. This was no laughing matter for the St Andrew's faithful. They were seeing their team being torn apart. It was embarrassing to say the least and in fact, as quite a few had turned up envisaging a place in the semi-finals for their team for the first time in thirty-one years. Not even the absence of nine first-team players was an excuse for their display in the early stages. It was absolutely horrid. Blues co-owner David Sullivan no doubt had a premonition when he wrote in the matchday programme: 'It would appear we have a mountain to climb.' His team had Everest standing in front of them after just 5 minutes.

The dangerous Crouch twice came close to adding a third before he once again found the back of the home net with his right foot in the 38th minute, after some terrific play by Luis Garcia. This triggered off some boisterous and rather unsavory behaviour from a section of irate Blues supporters. In fact, soon after that third Liverpool goal, a disgusted Birmingham fan slipped past the stewards and made his way towards manager Bruce in a scene similar to that which Steven McClaren had endured at Middlesbrough the previous month, when Aston Villa won 4-0 at the Riverside Stadium. The offender was duly escorted from the pitch, but not until he had made his feelings known to the watching gallery.

For Bruce, this was nothing short of humiliation by a rampant Liverpool side who should have scored twice more before half-time and again early in the second half. Chances were being created at regular intervals. The route to goal continued after the interval; Gerrard, Crouch (again) and John Arne Riise all going close before Spanish international Fernando Morientes, on as a substitute for Crouch, slotted home Liverpool's fourth from inside the 6-yard box after Steven Finnan, García and Gerrard had combined to slice open a disorientated Blues defence.

With 20 minutes remaining Riise joined the party, blasting home an unstoppable fifth goal. Blues had capitulated and more goals were on the cards. And, in fact, the Merseysiders hardly needed any help at this stage of a very one-sided contest, although Birmingham still obliged all the same, as defender Olivier Tébily turned Harry Kewell's cross into his own net with 13 minutes remaining.

23

FA CUP FINAL
LIVERPOOL 3 WEST HAM UNITED 3
(Reds won 3-1 on penalties)
13 May 2006

This was Liverpool's thirteenth appearance in the FA Cup final and it proved to be lucky!

They had previously played in the 1914, 1950, 1965, 1971, 1974, 1977, 1986, 1988, 1989, 1992, 1996 and 2001, winning the trophy six times and finishing runners-up on six occasions.

En route to this encounter with the Hammers at Cardiff's Millennium Stadium, the Reds had knocked out, Luton Town, Portsmouth, Manchester United, Birmingham City and Chelsea, while West Ham had accounted for Norwich City, Blackburn Rovers, Bolton Wanderers, Manchester City and Middlesbrough in that order.

Having finished third in the Premiership, nine points behind Chelsea and only one below Manchester United, Liverpool were perhaps favourites to beat the Hammers, who had ended their League season in ninth position. The Reds had also won both games between the clubs – 2-1 at Anfield and 2-0 at Upton Park.

Hammers' boss Alan Pardew was optimistic before the game, saying, 'This is a brand new ball game. We will go into the final with confidence ... we will let Liverpool do the worrying, but I wish we had a player like Steven Gerrard. If we had we would be favourites – not Liverpool.'

In contrast, Reds' boss Rafael Benítez said, 'We are in great form; we have won nine Premiership games on thee trot, scoring twenty-three goals and my players just can't wait to get started.'

Liverpool (4-4-2): Reina, Finnan, Hyypiä, Carragher, Riise, Gerrard, Sissoko, Alonso (Kromkamp), Kewell (Morientes); Cissé, Crouch (Hamann).
West Ham (4-4-2): Hislop, Scaloni, Ferdinand, Gabbidon, Konchesky Benayoun, Reo-Coker, Fletcher (Dailly), Etherington (Sheringham); Ashton (Zamora), Harewood.
Attendance: 71,140

On a swelteringly hot day, the support for Liverpool inside the stadium was absolutely superb, with banners, flags and scarves being swirled around by over

30,000 fans, most of whom had made the journey down from Merseyside. Let's be truthful, they were all expecting their team to win, but after half an hour West Ham were 2-0 up and looking comfortable.

After a fairly even start, Hammers' striker Dean Ashton was instrumental as West Ham stunned Liverpool by taking the lead after 21 minutes. His brilliant pass released overlapping right-back Lionel Scaloni, whose cross was unwittingly turned past his own goalkeeper, Pepe Reina, by the inrushing Jamie Carragher at the near post. Another error, this time by 'keeper Reina himself, handed West Ham a second goal just 6 minutes later.

Matthew Etherington's weak shot should have posed no problem for the Spanish 'keeper, but he fumbled the ball at the feet of Ashton, who had the simple task of bundling home from close range. At this point in the proceedings Liverpool were in desperate need of a rescue act. Xabi Alonso was so unsure of himself that he would later allow a simple pass to roll underneath his foot and was duly taken off and replaced by Dutchman Jan Kromkamp halfway through the second half, while Harry Kewell, another early substitution, never once attacked his marker, Scaloni and off he went too, replaced by Fernando Morientes in the 48th minute.

Then, quite unexpectedly really, up stepped a certain Steven Gerrard to drag Liverpool back into the game. Looking up, he deliberately picked out Djibril Cissé at the back post on 32 minutes and the French international did the rest. The Reds were back in the game. The match suddenly gathered momentum and Liverpool moved up a gear, West Ham slipped into reverse and although Marlon Harewood was denied by Reina seconds into the second half, it was that man Gerrard who hit the back of the net again, smashing home an equaliser 6 minutes before the hour mark from Peter Crouch's clever knock-down. Was this the cue for West Ham to collapse? No way. In fact, Pardew's side picked themselves up and came again.

In a rare attack, Paul Konchesky's speculative looping cross from the left on 64 minutes seemed to change its mind in mid-air and dipped over the back-pedalling Reina and into the net. Liverpool were behind once more, and with their supporters looking somewhat downhearted they knew they had to score again! There were a fewer close shaves, but realistically it was West Ham who came closest to increasing their lead, as Liverpool seemed to drop off the pace. As the clock slowly ticked down towards the 90 minute mark, Liverpool piled everyone forward and amazingly it was superhero Gerrard who proved to be the team's saviour yet again, as his first-time drive from 35 yards flew past Hislop's right hand and into the net. What a strike, what a goal. It was 3-3 and Liverpool – or rather Gerrard – had saved themselves.

In extra time, John Arne Riise almost scored a goal to rank alongside Gerrard's with a long-range effort that flew just over the angle, but it was West Ham who almost snatched victory with barely 90 seconds remaining of the 120, when Nigel Reo-Coker's deflected effort was turned on to the post by the diving Reina. A goalmouth scramble followed, before Harewood, who was suffering badly from cramp at this point, shot wide with an open goal at his mercy.

So to penalties – something Liverpool had been getting familiar with of late. Staffordshire referee Alan Wiley, who it must be said had very good game, spun the coin and Dietmar Hamann took the first kick for Liverpool and scored (1-0).

Zamora, who had been excellent throughout, then saw his 12-yard effort saved by Reina before Sami Hyypiä missed for Liverpool, Hislop saving low down. Next up it was the evergreen Teddy Sheringham, who comfortably found the net (1-1). The ever reliable Steven Gerrard then stepped forward to put Liverpool ahead at 2-1. Konchesky saw his kick saved by Reina and when Riise made it 3-1, atoning for his miss in the Champions League final against AC Milan, Anton Ferdinand knew he had to find the net with West Ham's fourth kick or it was game over. He looked nervous and Pepe Reina suddenly turned from villain to hero as he saved the defender's kick.

Liverpool had triumphed again from the 12-yard white spot. It was certainly tense stuff.

To sum up: Liverpool looked like the better side during extra time; they most certainly were in the penalty shoot-out. But the final belonged to Gerrard, who, for those of a militant Liverpudlian aspect, was the only royalty in Cardiff on 21 May 2006. His teammate Crouch said, 'It is always good to have a player like Stevie G in your team; he came up trumps again and we owe him so much. What a captain.'

Indeed, over the course of some 130 minutes, including three lots of added time, Gerrard was absolutely brilliant. Despite a bout of cramp, not to mention the exhaustion of the fifty-seven matches played during the season, his injury-time equaliser reminded Sam Wallace, reporting for the *Independent*, that 'He is certainly the player for the big occasion, a rare character, capable of imposing his might upon the most unpromising circumstances.'

It was a joyous, smiling Steven Gerrard – the Man of the Match by a country mile – who stepped forward to receive the coveted silver trophy from HRH Prince William, who was just as happy to get his hands on the Cup as the Liverpool skipper!

In the best traditions of the FA Cup, with time moving on, there were at least six injured players who were unable to leave the field because all the substitutes had come on; cramp attacks were striking players all over the pitch but they all battled on, showing great commitment.

24

FA COMMUNITY SHIELD
CHELSEA 1 LIVERPOOL 2
13 August 2006

There will never be a better way to start a season than to win a piece of silverware, and Liverpool did just that at what had become their second home – the Millennium Stadium in Cardiff.

Three new boys were all ready to make their debuts – striker Craig Bellamy (signed from Blackburn Rovers for £6 million), wide midfielder Jermaine Pennant (who cost £6.7 million from Birmingham City) and defender Fabio Aurelio (recruited on a Bosman free transfer from Valencia). These new signings, along with midfielders Steven Gerrard and Xabi Alonso on the bench, there was certainly an air of optimism among the huge gathering of Anfield support inside the sun-drenched Welsh arena.

Chelsea were at full strength, with manager José Mourinho fielding two new recruits in his starting line-up – Andrey Shevchenko (who cost a cool £30.8 million) and the experienced German Michael Ballack. 'The Special One' in fact, was quietly confident that his team would win, saying before kick-off: 'I always like to beat Liverpool and I feel we will do just that today.'

Chelsea (4-4-2): Cudicini, Paulo Ferreira (Mikel), Terry, Carvalho, Essien, Geremi (Bridge), Ballack (Kalou), Lampard, Shevchenko, Drogba (Wright-Phillips), Robben (Diarra).
Liverpool: Reina, Finnan, Agger, Carragher, Riise, Pennant (Gerrard), Sissoko, Zenden (Alonso), Gonzalez (Aurelio), Crouch (Sinama Pongolle), Luis Garcia (Bellamy).
Attendance: 56,275

The game started off rather slowly with both sides sparring against each other, but then it burst into life as early as the 9th minute. The Chelsea supporters were still admiring the way Shevchenko had pressurized the Liverpool defence into conceding a corner when they saw their team fall behind.

Right-back Steven Finnan headed the ball clear and it fell conveniently to John Arne Riise just outside his own penalty area, to the right area. Taking control, he ran some 80 yards downfield virtually unchallenged, before unleashing a 25-yard left footed shot which realistically the Chelsea goalkeeper, Carlo Cudicini, should have saved. He didn't, and it was 1-0 to the Reds.

Standing up, arms folded and staring at his defenders, Mourinho looked on in disgust, muttering to himself. He was not at all happy with the way his back line simply parted company and left a gaping gap in which Riise charged into before delivering his fine goal. In stark contrast, Mourinho's counterpart, 'Rafa the Gaffa', in the Liverpool dug-out, was absolutely delighted – and why shouldn't he be?

Then, as Chelsea slowly but surely forced themselves back into the game, Mourinho's mood worsened even more as first Frank Lampard was booked for a petulant kick on Bolo Zenden and then debutant Ballack, who had been yellow-carded after just 7 minutes, hobbled off with an apparent hip injury shortly before the half-hour mark, to be replaced by Soloman Kalou.

Liverpool had a great chance to go 2-0 up in the 35th minute when the lively Mark Gonzalez fired a low, dangerous cross between the Chelsea goalposts and the edge of the penalty area goal. The ball, in fact, deflected off Luis Garcia and the alert Cudicini reacted quickly to tip it over the bar while under pressure from Peter Crouch.

Chelsea were struggling to get any rhythm into their play. Lampard and Kalou were certainly second best in midfield and Liverpool looked well in control as half-time approached. But, out of blue to some for sure, Chelsea's new Ukrainian international Shevchenko pulled his side level on 43 minutes. The seemingly ineffective Lampard somehow managed to push a forward pass through to his striker who controlled the ball superbly before coolly slotting it low past Pepe Reina. The Shevchenko show continued in the second half and the former AC Milan striker, who was given too much space, forced Reina into a fine one-handed save from his well-directed header.

Chelsea looked a different team to what they had been in the first period, and as they began to take charge of proceedings Benítez introduced both Gerrard and Alonso into the action for the last 30 minutes, soon afterwards bringing on Bellamy. As the pendulum started to swing Liverpool's way, Gerrard (twice), Crouch, Bellamy and Riise all tested Cudicin. In the end it was a Welsh striker, Craig Bellamy making his club debut at the Millennium Stadium, who made the difference in the end.

With 10 minutes remaining on referee Martin Atkinson's watch and the game seemingly drifting towards extra time, Bellamy's electric pace saw him break clear down the left. Looking up, the sprightly forward engineered enough space to deliverer a fabulous high cross which Crouch, timing is run and leap to perfection, headed home in style at the far post. Liverpool's Brazilian substitute Aurelio might even have made the score-line look more emphatic, but he was denied a goal by affine diving save by Cudicini late on. Chelsea had nothing more to offer after falling behind and Liverpool held on comfortably to lift the pre-season annual trophy for the tenth time outright.

According to the adjudicators, none of the three players who found the net did enough during the game to scoop the Man of the Match award. That accolade went to Liverpool's workhorse supreme, Momo Sissoko, who ran the midfield to produce one of his best-ever performance in a red shirt. Afterwards Gerrard said, 'He was terrific, outstanding in fact. I never thought he had it in him!'

25

CHAMPIONS LEAGUE FINAL
AC MILAN 2 LIVERPOOL 1
23 May 2007

Despite victory in the Community Shield game against Chelsea, Rafa Benítez saw Liverpool have a difficult start to the season. Thankfully they recovered and went on to reach a second Champions League final in three years. For this achievement alone, the accusations of Lucky Liverpool started to fade away. Liverpool lacked consistency in the Premiership and ended up finishing third, similar to what Milan achieved. In fact, they were effectively out of the Serie A title race by Christmas, but in the New Year they battened down the hatches and focused on the Champions League and it paid off big time!

Liverpool began their route to the final by knocking out Maccabi Haifi 3-2 on aggregate in the third qualifying round. They then played six games in Group C, gaining four wins, one draw and one defeat, before knocking out over two legs: Barcelona on the away goal rule (courtesy of an excellent 2-1 victory at the Nou Camp), PSV Eindhoven (4-0 on aggregate) and Chelsea (4-1 on penalties after a 1-1 stalemate in the semi-final).

Initially Milan took care of Red Star Belgrade in a qualifying tie (3-1 over two games) before winning three, drawing one and losing two of their Group H matches, squeezing past Lille and AEK Athens to make it through to the knockout stage. They then successfully eliminated Celtic (1-0 over two legs), Bayern Munich (4-2 on aggregate) and Manchester United (5-3 overall).

AC Milan (4-4-1-1): Dida, Oddo, Nesta, Maldini, Jankulovski (Kaladze), Gattuso, Pirlo, Ambrosini, Seedorf (Favelli), Kaka, Inzaghi (Gilardino).
Liverpool (4-2-3-1): Reina, Finnan (Arboleo), Agger, Carragher, Riise, Pennant, Macharerano (Crouch), Alonso, Gerrard, Zenden (Kewell), Kuyt.
Attendance: 74,000

The Olympic Stadium in Athens was the venue for this eagerly awaited England-Italy showdown, a repeat of the terrific 2005 final which Liverpool won on penalties after coming back from 3-0 down.

Liverpool, winning the toss, kicked off and threatened straightaway, but Jermaine Pennant just could not reach Steven Gerrard's probing cross-field pass.

Milan responded quickly, aiming two counter-attacks towards Pepe Reina's goal, but reliable defender Jamie Carragher was able to clear them both. The second clearance, however, led to a corner, which saw Milan send six players into the penalty area; the Reds' back-line held firm and the danger was cleared.

Liverpool had the first chance of the match in the 9th minute. A slip by Milan defender Marek Jankulovski allowed Pennant to run into space. He exchanged passes with Dutchman Dirk Kuyt, but Pennant's subsequent shot was saved low down by Milan goalkeeper Dida. Minutes later Gerrard won a header that found Pennant, however Stevie G was unable to make decent contact with the ball following his colleague's clever pass.

Milan's first effort of the match came on 20 minutes. The Brazilian Kaká received a short pass just outside the area and after moving the ball from his left foot to his right, his tame shot was easily saved by Reina. Liverpool continued to exert pressure and this led to a mistake by Milan defender Massimo Oddo, who completely misjudged a cross from Pennant, allowing the ball to reach Gerrard whose shot sailed over the bar.

The Reds almost carved out a clear chance in the 27th minute and it took some frantic defending before Xabi Alonso fired wide of the goal. A mistake by Jankulovski then allowed Gerrard to feed Kuyt inside the penalty area, but his shot was blocked by defender Alessandro Nesta. Milan midfielder Gennaro Gattuso was yellow-carded in the 40th minute for a foul on Alonso and soon afterwards came the breakthrough for the Italians. Alonso was lucky not to receive a caution when he fouled Kaká on the edge of the Liverpool area. The evergreen Andrea Pirlo delivered a menacing free-kick, which deflected off the shoulder (actually upper arm) of his own teammate Filippo Inzaghi, and past the flat-footed Reina who was diving the other way.

Inzaghi later said that while the deflection was intended he did not mean for the ball to hit his arm. Oh yes.

2 minutes into the second half, Nesta tackled Gerrard before he could reach Kuyt's pass and a lucky Jankuloski received only a yellow card in the 54th minute after bringing down Pennant.

Immediately afterwards, Pirlo crossed high to Kaká who was fractionally offside, before but Liverpool defender Daniel Agger produced a tremendous tackle on Inzaghi just as he was about to pull the trigger.

Liverpool had their first yellow card in the 59th minute when Javier Mascherano was booked for bringing down Pirlo and straightway Boudewijn Zenden was replaced by Harry Kewell. Liverpool then created their best scoring chance of the match to that point. The busy figure of Gerrard capitalised on an error by Gattuso to gain a one-on-one on goalkeeper Dida, but his shot lacked power to beat the Milan shot-stopper. Encouraged by this, Liverpool began to exert more pressure, but their play lacked penetration despite Milan being unable to retain possession.

With time ticking on, Rafael Benítez took off Mascherano and brought on Peter Crouch, but before the lanky striker could make any worthwhile contribution, Milan scored a second goal. Kaká, in ample space, found time to pick out striker Inzaghi, who took the ball to the side of the Liverpool goalkeeper Reina before rolling it into the unguarded net. This was a body blow, but backed by their vociferous fans, Liverpool managed to pull a goal back in the 88th minute when Kuyt scored after Agger had flicked on Pennant's well-driven corner.

However, with every AC Milan player bedded behind the ball for the remaining few minutes, Liverpool simply couldn't find a way through to score again before efficient German referee Herbert Fandel ended the contest.

Milan manager Carlo Ancelotti was obviously delighted with his team's performance, saying, 'When I think back to December when I was almost sacked, we had to overcome so many hurdles so that makes it a very special victory.' Liverpool boss Rafael Benítez was very disappointed and upset that his players were unable to match their exploits of 2005. He said, 'I'm still proud of them. You could see the quality they had ... we need to start thinking how we can improve our team.'

Steven Gerrard was adamant that despite the defeat Liverpool would come back stronger next season: 'We've got to pick ourselves up, have a good rest in the summer and then go again next season.' He thought that although Liverpool were in control during the first 45 minutes – they had 58 per cent of the play – they did not control the second half as they would have liked. He also echoed his manager's sentiments with regard to the signing of new players: 'We need to strengthen and bring some quality into the club. The manager and the people in charge of the club know that and it will be an interesting summer.'

For the record, Milan midfielder Clarence Seedorf collected his fourth winners' medal in this competition and no less than thirteen players – seven from Milan and six from Liverpool – had appeared in the 2005 Champions League final.

Ticket Problems

Only 9,000 tickets for this final went on general sale; the remainder was shared between the two teams who got 17,000 each, while the UEFA family and sponsors received 20,800 tickets. There were many problems before the match. In fact, minutes before kick-off, scores of fans were still queuing to gain entry to the stadium. At this point it is understood that the Greek police informed them that the ground was full and denied entry to approximately 5,000 supporters who had genuine tickets.

Riot police arrived on the scene and using tear gas and batons tried to disperse the crowd. UEFA spokesman William Gaillard subsequently blamed Liverpool fans for causing the problems, stating: 'Milan supporters didn't face the same problems because they didn't behave in the same way.' A further UEFA report released soon after the final branded Liverpool fans 'the worst in Europe', with Gaillard stating: 'What other set of fans steal tickets from their fellow supporters or out of the hands of children?'

However, UEFA President Michel Platini later denied that Liverpool fans were the worst behaved in Europe and said that the trouble was down to 'poor ticket-checking procedures and for implementing insufficient measures to deal with the large number of fans'. Simon Gass, the British ambassador to Greece, said, 'Clearly there was some element of breakdown where those fake tickets appeared to be legitimate – that's something UEFA must look at.'

Meanwhile, Liverpool's co-owner Tom Hicks described UEFA's allocation of 17,000 tickets to each team, knowing that Liverpool would be bringing 40,000 supporters, as 'insane', and accused Gaillard of blaming Liverpool fans in order to cover up for his own mistakes. UEFA was further criticised by both participating clubs, AC Milan and Liverpool, for their lack of provision for the clubs' disabled fans, providing the clubs with only sixteen disabled tickets each.

26

CHAMPIONS LEAGUE
LIVERPOOL 8 BESIKTAS 0
6 November 2007

After Marseille had suffered a surprise defeat at the hands of FC Porto, victory over Besiktas would see Liverpool climb into third place in Group A of their Champions League campaign, just three points short of the second qualifying place with two fixtures remaining. As it was, Rafael Benítez's side and Marseille could finish level on ten points each in the group if both won their next matches and Liverpool then triumphed (at least by 1-0) in France, having lost by that score at Anfield earlier in the season. So, effectively it was all down to the number of goals scored and therefore it was imperative that Liverpool should fire a few past the Turks ... and they did just that!

Liverpool (4-4-2): Reina, Aurelio (Babel), Hyypiä, Carragher, Arbeloa, Riise, Mascherano, Gerrard (Lucas), Benayoun, Voronin (Kewell), Crouch.
Besiktas (4-5-1): Arikan, Uzulmez, Toraman, Diatta, Kurtulus (Higuain), Sedef (Ricardinho), Cisse, Avci, Ozcan (Tandogan), Delgado, Bobo.
Attendance: 41,143

Prior to kick-off, Liverpool had netted only two goals in their group. So no pressure then on Steven Gerrard and his players as they went out, sleeves rolled up and ready for action.

German referee Markus Merk got the gamed underway and right from the start there was only going to be one winner – the team in red! The Turks were well and truly battered with clemency nowhere to be found.

Benítez, who deliberately selected an attacking line-up, had the Argentina Javier Mascherano anchoring the midfield while his teammates concentrated on overpowering Besiktas with aggressive, total commitment and the desire to win. Despite all the pyrotechnics this turned out to be a mature display, with Liverpool methodically building their dominance prior to the interval. In effect Besiktas were outclassed, although Liverpool found themselves only two goals in front after barely half an hour had been completed. Besiktas, minus their best defender, rugged centre-back Gokhan Zan, ultimately surrendered to despair.

After dominating the opening exchanges – although Mehmet Sedef did shoot wide for the visitors – it was Peter Crouch who initially nudged Besiktas towards capitulation. Ukrainian Andriy Voronin aimed a forward pass towards the lanky striker on 19 minutes and, when holding midfielder Edouard Cissé tried to intercept, he only managed to divert the ball into the path of Crouch, whose first attempt was saved by the hapless goalkeeper Hakan Arikan. With the defenders static, however, the striker had the simple task knocking of in the rebound.

With 32 minutes gone the visitors should have been awarded a throw-in after the ball went out of play off John Arne Riise, but the Norwegian shamelessly took it himself and found Voronin, who crossed deep towards Yossi Benayoun who, in space, took two touches before finishing well with a crisp, low drive. Besiktas, disheartened, became ever more fragile and even without Voronin in terrific form, Liverpool would surely have comfortably beaten tougher visitors than the Turkish champions. Voronin's energy was stunning and before half-time he twice went close to scoring himself, as did Gerrard, Crouch again and also Riise.

8 minutes into the second half, Man of the Match Voronin set up Riise, whose bullet-like drive was pushed away by Arikan but only went as far as Benayoun, who, taking aim, fired in his second goal of the night to give Liverpool a 3-0 lead. The Israeli was now eager to complete his hat-trick and he achieved that in the 56th minute.

Lamine Diatta clumsily brought down Voronin and from Gerrard's precise free-kick, the ball came back off the goalkeeper to the waiting Benayoun, who bulged the net from close range.

Liverpool were on fire, the fans were roaring and Besiktas had given up! 4-0 became 5-0 in the 69th minute when Gerrard, after completing clever one-twos with both Mascherano and Voronin, who delivered a smart back-heeler, smashed his shot past a deflated Arikan who simply shrugged his shoulders, mumbling to his defenders! With the opposition in total disarray, Dutch star Ryan Babel (a mid-second-half substitute for Aurelio) bagged Liverpool's sixth goal when he audaciously flicked in a Benayoun cut-back with the inside of his heel on 79 minutes.

2 minutes later Ibrahim Toraman's clearance bounced off Babel who had charged down a long downfield punt, and the ball floated high into the net over the stranded Arikjean. With time running out, and Babel reveling in the atmosphere, he even had time to head against the crossbar before Crouch glanced in a header from a Benayoun measured cross. This completed the rout with 90 seconds remaining and gave Liverpool their biggest ever win in the Champions League.

NB: Liverpool were subsequently dragged into the match-fixing scandal after this victory that rocked European football. Reports were made that this record Champions League was considered suspicious because of irregular betting patterns. UEFA officials refused to confirm or deny the allegations at the time, but the saga roiled on for a short while before everything died down.

27

CHAMPIONS LEAGUE QUARTER FINAL, 2ND LEG
LIVERPOOL 4 ARSENAL 2
8 April 2008

After coming through a difficult group stage and then knocking out Inter Milan, Liverpool drew Arsenal in the last eight of the Champions League. It looked a tough assignment on paper and so it proved.

The first leg at the Emirates finished level at 1-1, with Emmanuel Adebayor and Dirk Kuyt scoring the respective goals and making the return game at Anfield something to look forward to. Liverpool had the slight advantage, courtesy of that vital away goal on Merseyside, but Steven Gerrard was taking nothing for granted, saying, 'Anything can happen in a football match, and we shall go out with confidence of course, but we will all be aware of what Arsenal are capable of. They have some fine players and I know it will be a tough game.'

Liverpool (4-4-2): Reina, Carragher, Skrtel, Hyypiä, Aurelio, Gerrard, Alonso, Mascherano, Kuyt (Arbeloa), Torres (Riise), Crouch (Babel).
Arsenal (4-4-2): Almunia, Toure, Gallas, Senderos, Clichy, Eboue (Walcott), Flamini (Silva), Fabregas, Diaby (Van Persie), Hleb, Adebayor.
Attendance: 41, 985

In front of almost 42,000 fans, Liverpool and Arsenal produced a cracking game of football on April 2008. In the end it was the hosts who came out on top with a late flourish to set up another Champions League semi-final encounter with their now arch-rivals in knockout competitions – Chelsea.

Abou Diaby gave Arsenal an early lead but centre-back Sami Hyypiä lost Phillipe Senderos at a set piece to head home an equaliser. Spanish striker Fernando Torres then looked to have settled the contest in Liverpool's favour when he cracked the ball home with aplomb into the top corner of the Gunners' net, but a superb Theo Walcott run allowed Emmanuel Adebayor to tap in an unlikely equaliser.

Thankfully, Liverpool found an extra gear and when Kolo Toure fouled substitute Ryan Babel, Stevie G held his nerve to find the net from the spot. Soon after, Babel broke clear to add a fourth and seal a 5-3 aggregate victory for Rafael Benítez's men. Let it be known, it was an extraordinary end to yet another superbly entertaining European contest at Anfield. The two sides, who had already faced each other twice in the previous five days, saved their best for this third battle of the 'Reds'. The game itself was full of drama from the first whistle to the last.

Both teams, with attack firmly in mind played as if their season was on the line and it resulted in a pulsating cup tie. Arsenal came out of the blocks looking like they had a new lease of life from the side that began proceedings so lethargically in the Premiership encounter over the previous weekend, so it came as no surprise when they went ahead through Diaby, who had been recalled by manager Arsene Wenger.

The French midfielder burst into the 18-yard box to collect Alexander Hleb's measured pass before driving home a well-struck, low shot that Pepe Reina, in all honesty, may have saved but could only help the ball into the net.

This timely goal seemed to inject more gusto into Arsenal's play and as a result it was Liverpool, the home side, who were beginning to look somewhat jaded! The Gunners created and missed a couple of chances and in the end they were made to pay for not adding to their opening goal. After half an hour, centre-half Philippe Senderos was caught flat footed, allowing Hyypiä the freedom of the Anfield penalty box to head firmly past Manuel Almunia from a fine cross by Cesc Fabregas, the ball flying in off the post.

Now it was Liverpool's turn to dictate the play and after Gerrard and Kuyt had both gone close, either side of half-time, their dominance finally paid off midway through the second period. Manager Benítez's decision to partner the lanky Peter Crouch with Torres up front had looked initially like a tactical blunder as they failed to gel at all during the early stages of the match, but it was a pairing that was to combine excellently for Liverpool's second goal. Crouch's clever flick was latched onto by Torres, who turned and shot in an instant to send the Kop into delirium.

Arsenal responded quickly and Emmanuel Adebayor was only just off target with a desperate lunge from Emmanuel Eboue's cross, but everyone inside Anfield knew that the visitors were, at this stage, looking increasingly desperate, on the ropes as Liverpool pressed again. However, Wenger brought on substitute Theo Walcott in the 72nd minute (for the tiring Eboue) and straightaway his presence seemed to revitalize the flagging Gunners. Hovering in his own half of the field, he looked around and, after collecting the ball, set off a brilliant mazy dribble that saw him beat six Liverpool defenders in a magical run, before he squared the ball into the path of his teammate Adebayor who was able to side foot home from close range, giving Reina no chance whatsoever.

Liverpool were stunned, but urged on by Gerrard and roared on by their supporters they regrouped and immediately went down the other end of the field where substitute Marcus Babel was brought tumbling down inside the box by Toure. Penalty said referee Peter Frojdfeldt, from Sweden. No way, said the Arsenal players, who were furious at the decision. But as cool as a cucumber, up stepped the ever reliable Stevie G to score from the spot, firing the ball high into the top corner with just 4 minutes left on the clock.

An Arsenal response at that stage would have been enough to send them through on away goals and they threw everyone forward in a bold attempt to score again. But with acres of space at the back, it was no surprise when the pacy Babel raced clear to slot home Liverpool's fourth goal of the night and ease the pain of that rather contentious penalty decision.

It was a cruel exit for Arsenal but there was no denying it was Liverpool's night. They played very well with Gerrard giving an outstanding performance.

Next up it was Chelsea in the two-legged semi-final – the third time in four years the teams had met in the competition. And everyone wanted a ticket to see another 'Clash of the Titans'.

28

CHAMPIONS LEAGUE, SEMI-FINAL 2ND LEG
CHELSEA 3 LIVERPOOL 2
(lost 4-3 on aggregate)
30 April 2008

This was a big, big game and everyone associated with Liverpool – the players, coaching staff, the entire management, directors and supporters alike – knew it. It would be tense, and having drawn the first leg 1-1 at Anfield when John Arne Riise conceded a late own goal, Chelsea were regarded as clear favourites to make it through the final. Liverpool boss Rafael Benítez said, 'It would be like a cup final itself at Stamford Bridge' and Steven Gerrard added, 'As the away team the onus will be on Chelsea and although have an away goal advantage, we will score I'm sure, and then it will be all to play for.'

En route to the semi-finals, Liverpool had finished second in Group A behind FC Porto (11 points to ten). They then took on, and knocked out, Inter Milan (2-0, 1-1) and Arsenal (1-1, 4-2) to set up a two-legged showdown with the Blues.

Chelsea (4-5-1): Čech, Essien, Carvalho, Terry, A. Cole, J. Cole (Anelka), Ballack, Makelele, Lampard (Shevchenko), Kalou (Malouda), Drogba.
Liverpool (4-5-1): Reina, Arbeloa, Carragher, Skrtel (Hyypiä), Riise, Kuyt, Alonso, Mascherano, Benayoun (Pennant), Gerrard, Torres (Babel).
Attendance: 38,900

Like everyone thought and anticipated, this turned out to be a tight game and in the end it was disappointment for Steven Gerrard and Liverpool as Chelsea achieved their dream of gaining a place in the UEFA Champions League final.

On a night of high drama and shear emotion, this second-leg encounter went to extra time, during which Didier Drogba scored his second goal of the night after Frank Lampard, making his return to action following the untimely death of his mother, had swung the tie back Chelsea's way by converting a penalty.

In the end it was sweet revenge for the Blues over the Reds, who had proved their nemesis at this stage of the competition on two previous occasions in the space of three seasons. Drogba had given Chelsea a first-half lead on 33 minutes, Fernando Torres (playing against his future club) equalised just 9 minutes after the interval and after Lampard (with his penalty on 98 minutes) and Drogba (again, 105) had put the home side 3-1 in front. Ryan Babel then bagged a late goal but to no avail for the Reds.

Chelsea were clearly not at all interested in sitting on their advantage of their vital away goal from the first leg. After 24 hours of incessant rain, the surface at the Bridge proved troublesome, yet crucially Chelsea seemed to keep their feet far better than their opponents. Their passes were more precise and assured, and early on Drogba, steering away from Jamie Carragher, crashed in a powerful drive that Pepe Reina pushed aside. Liverpool struck back quickly and when Yossi Benayoun found Steven Gerrard, the midfielder set Torres clear, but home 'keeper Petr Čech was swiftly off his line to smother the Spaniard's low shot.

Chelsea continued to control the game and Reina had to sprint off his line to thwart Drogba, who then somehow dragged another effort wide after Lampard had fed him with an excellent pass. Unfortunately, Liverpool lost centre-back Martin Škrtel in the 22nd minute. He hobbled off with a leg injury and was replaced by Sami Hyypiä.

At this point, the Reds were under some pressure and it came as no surprise when Chelsea took the lead just past the half-hour mark. Salomon Kalou stretched the defence down the left and forced Reina into a flying save. Before any Liverpool player could react, Drogba was first on the scene to rifle home an unstoppable shot, the ball flying in at the near post.

Liverpool started the second half on the front foot and only Čech's outstretched left leg kept Chelsea's lead intact. From a well-executed free-kick, Gerrard headed on to Dirk Kuyt, whose delicate flick was heading in before the tall goalkeeper intervened. Despite looking good, Liverpool's expected onslaught continued and, in the 64th minute, Benayoun set off on a driving run that took him past four defenders, before his prodded pass found Torres who finished well with a low shot into the bottom corner of Čech's goal. The Spanish striker almost worked another opening as Liverpool sought to exploit their advantage, although Chelsea's midfielder Michael Essien came closest to averting extra time, shooting into the side-netting from an acute angle.

The additional 30 minutes started at a breathless pace. Hyypiä headed wide for Liverpool before Essien saw his goal ruled out for offside by a teammate. When Hyypiä's mistimed lunge brought the German Michael Ballack tumbling down in the 98th minute, Italian referee Roberto Rosetti immediately pointed to the penalty spot. Up stepped the cool-headed figure of Lampard who converted, right-footed, before breaking down in tears amid a huddle of jubilant colleagues.

Liverpool were shell-shocked. Passes started to go astray, tackles were missed and it was virtually all over when Drogba, getting in front of Jamie Carragher and Alvaro Arbeloa, expertly turned in Nicolas Anelka's low centre in the 105th minute. Liverpool managed to conjure up one more worthwhile attack and with 3 minutes remaining Ryan Babel found the net with a 35-yard rocket.

The Londoners, however, pulled everyone back behind the ball and held firm, denying Liverpool the chance to pressurize Čech's goal, and soon afterwards the final whistle triggered off wild celebrations inside Stamford Bridge as Stevie G and his disappointed teammates made their way to the dressing room. 'We fought hard; we gave it everything we had; we are gutted; but that's football', said a despondent Stevie G.

Chelsea, managed by Avram Grant, met Sir Alex Ferguson's Manchester United in the final in Moscow, and following a 1-1 after 120 minutes, United won the resulting penalty shoot-out 6-5.

29

PREMIER LEAGUE
CHELSEA 0 LIVERPOOL 1
26 October 2008

Chelsea, undefeated at home in eighty-six matches, were confident of extending their superb record at Stamford Bridge against Liverpool, but the Reds were also quietly confident themselves of ending the Blues' run and so leap to the top of the Premiership. Manager Rafael Benítez chose to flood midfield, playing only Robbie Keane up front, in a bold effort to outwit and, indeed, out manoeuvre the Londoners. His astute plan paid off.

Chelsea (4-4-2): Čech, Bosingwa (Sinclair), Carvalho, Terry, Ashley Cole, Mikel, Kalou (Di Santo), Deco, Lampard, Malouda (Belletti), Anelka.
Liverpool (4-5-1): Reina, Arbeloa, Carragher, Agger, Aurelio, Alonso, Mascherano, Kuyt (Lucas), Gerrard, Riera (Hyypiä), Keane (Babel).
Attendance: 41,705

This was a tight game, pretty tense at times, but in the end Liverpool – without key striker Fernando Torres – prevailed, courtesy of fellow Spaniard Xabi Alonso's deflected 10th minute goal that ended Chelsea's quite supreme sequence of home results which had started four and a half years earlier, in February 2004. It was a thoroughly deserved triumph for Rafael Benítez's side, while at the same time it was the first real setback for the reign of Chelsea boss, Luiz Felipe Scolari. Victory certainly boosted Liverpool's confidence and, indeed, self-belief.

There is no doubt that Chelsea enjoyed long periods of possession, but Liverpool always looked threatening, never shirking a tackle and ready to con test every loose ball. In fact, they could easily have doubled their winning margin had Alonso's second-half free-kick not struck an upright.

England left-back Ashley Cole missed Chelsea's best chance, which didn't materialize until after the break, clearly emphasizing how well Liverpool defended. Liverpool played well and many thought that they must now be considered as serious title contenders, finally having the overall ability to challenge Chelsea and Manchester United in the battle for domestic honours. There is no doubt that

Chelsea simply ran out of ideas and steam, unable to penetrate Liverpool's red wall of resistance that was marshalled magnificently by Jamie Carragher.

Chelsea started well enough but were stunned when Alonso struck to give Liverpool the lead. The midfielder latched on to a half-clearance and, although his effort carried little power, the ball deflected off José Bosingwa and completely wrong-footed a stranded Petr Čech in the home goal.

Chelsea steadied the ship and tried to restore the balance by dominating possession but Liverpool were superbly organized, with Steven Gerrard, Alonso and Javier Mascherano working overtime in centre-field, competing for every ball, while behind them Carragher and co. looked impregnable, and Robbie Keane in particular always looked capable of sneaking a second goal on the break. Stevie G almost found then net in the 23rd minute but his dipping effort from 25 yards was finger-tipped to safety by the diving Čech. Mascherano was protecting his back four brilliantly and with the atmosphere inside Stamford Bridge rather subdued as far as the home supporters were concerned, the travelling Liverpool fans were seeing their team producing the goods.

10 minutes before the interval, and certainly out of the blue, Deco almost provided an equalizer. Gerrard lost possession and the Portugal midfielder advanced towards Pepe Reina's goal before fizzing a fierce left-footer inches wide.

Chelsea had obviously enjoyed the majority of possession in the first 45 minutes and they continued to do so during the early stages of the second half, but the resilient Liverpool stuck in there and if the truth be known, goalkeeper Reina was not seriously tested.

Gerrard was pushed into a more advanced role to support Keane but straightaway there was a moment of anxiety for Reina when, on 54 minutes, he clumsily brought down Florent Malouda inside the penalty area. Thankfully, the Spaniard escaped punishment when he learned that the linesman's flag had already been raised for offside.

That was the Chelsea player's final contribution as manager Scolari made a double change, bringing on Franco di Santo and Juliano Belletti while also taking off Salomon Kalou. Liverpool took off Keane and introduced Ryan Babel and almost immediately they came close to adding a second goal when Alonso's well-directed free-kick left Čech motionless, but the ball cannoned off the base of the post and stayed out.

Cole, having already been booked, should have received a second yellow after a reckless foul on Babel, but Mascherano's stupid intervention in an attempt to ensure he was sent off resulted in a booking for the Argentine instead!

Liverpool had pressurised Chelsea in every department, and as the clock started to tick down on their formidable home record, some of the home players began to lose their composure and belief. They still managed to carve out an opening on 72 minutes, but the unmarked Cole sliced his effort hopelessly wide after Di Santo had steered Frank Lampard's cross into his path. Carragher then threw his whole body

1. Stevie G celebrating after scoring against Real Madrid in a Champions League game in March 2009.

2. Looking rather disappointed after coming close to scoring against Borussia Dortmund in a Champions League game in 2001.

3. Daniel Agger and Steven Gerrard.

4. Steven Gerrard applauds the crowd after a Group B Champions League match between Real Madrid and Liverpool at the Santiago Bernabeu stadium in Madrid, Spain, 4 November 2014. (*Courtesy of Press Association*)

5. Steven Gerrard is challenged by Ludogorets' Cosmin Moti during the Champions League Group B soccer match between Ludogorets and Liverpool at Vassil Levski stadium in Sofia, Bulgaria, November 2014. (*Courtesy of Press Association*)

6. Steven Gerrard warms up before kick-off during the UEFA Champions League Group B match on 4 November 2014 at the Santiago Bernabeu, Madrid, Spain. (*Courtesy of Press Association*)

7. Steven Gerrard relaxing before the game against AS Roma at Fenway Park in July 2012.

8. Steven Gerrard is somewhat dejected after Liverpool's 2-1 Champions League final defeat to AC Milan in the Olympic Stadium in Athens in 2007. (*Courtesy of Press Association*)

9. Steven Gerrard scoring against AC Milan in the UEFA Champions League final in May 2005. (*Courtesy of Press Association*)

forward to block Deco's shot, while at the other end of the field Babel produced a rising drive that flew just inches wide.

Chelsea pushed seven players forward in the closing stages, but not in a convincing manner, allowing Liverpool's defence to easily cope with any threatening situations. When referee Howard Webb blew the final whistle, it was arms raised, hugs and celebrations by the Liverpool players who, with this hard-earned victory, moved three points clear of Chelsea at the top of the Premiership.

Man of the Match Stevie G said afterwards, 'We deserved that. We were up for it from the start. This was a great result.'

30

PREMIER LEAGUE
BLACKBURN ROVERS 1 LIVERPOOL 3
6 December 2008

Paul Ince, manager of Blackburn Rovers, was quietly confident that his team could beat his former employers at Ewood Park, despite being on a run of nine games without a win in all competitions. At the time, Rovers were lying second from bottom in the Premiership and were desperately in need of points, whereas Liverpool – who had recently gone to the top the pile – went into the game looking to rediscover their shooting boots after drawing blanks in their last two games, both at Anfield, against Fulham and West Ham United.

Reds' boss Rafa Benítez knew he would be without striker Fernando Torres, who was struggling with an irritating hamstring injury, and had to decide whether or not to use Robbie Keane up front once again. In the end he went for Kuyt and Babel, but chose Steven Gerrard to push further forward to support the front two, leaving Javier Mascherano to return to the engine room as anchorman. Full-back Fabio Aurelio was also sidelined with a calf problem. Blackburn, who had lost to Manchester United in a mid-week League Cup tie, were thankful that both Roque Santa Cruz and Brett Emerton were passed fit to play.

Blackburn Rovers (4-4-2): Robinson, Ooijer, Samba, Nelsen, Warnock, Emerton, Andrews, Pedersen (McCarthy), Derbyshire (Treacey), Tugay (Vogel), Santa Cruz. **Liverpool** (4-2-3-1): Reina, Arbeloa, Carragher, Hyypiä, Insua, Benayoun (Riera), Mascherano (Lucas), Alonso, Gerrard, Babel (El Zhar), Kuyt. **Attendance:** 26,920

Although in the end Liverpool won comfortably, their overall performance was not good – far from it! They were disappointing for the majority of the first two thirds of the game and their performance only improved after Spaniard Xabi Alonso had opened the scoring for the Reds in the 68th minute. The hardworking Yossi Benayoun looked to have secured victory 11 minutes later, but a fine strike from Roque Santa Cruz produced a nail-biting finale before Steven Gerrard whipped in the clinching goal in injury time.

Let's be truthful, the first half provided very little goalmouth action as far as Liverpool were concerned; what did happen came from Blackburn! In fact, Liverpool were caught cold as early as the 6th minute when the Dane, Morten

Gamst Pedersen, found space inside the penalty area, but only succeeded in delivering his misguided cross into the arms of goalkeeper José Reina, much to the disbelief and certainly the annoyance of the home supporters! Rovers' rugged Turkish forward Kerimoğlu Tugay then attempted to release Santa Cruz, but put far too much weight on the pass and Reina was able to make a well-timed interception.

It had been an encouraging start by Blackburn and on 13 minutes Pedersen whipped over a corner, but Santa Cruz's touch let him down with an open goal in front of him. Surprisingly, Liverpool almost took the lead in their first attack on 19 minutes. Dirk Kuyt spotted Benayoun running deep into the Rovers' half. He found him with an exquisite through ball but covering left-back Stephen Warnock was able stretch out his leg and nick the ball off the foot of the Israeli midfielder as he shaped to shoot. Warnock got a pat on the back from his goalkeeper Robinson, for what was a brilliantly timed and crucial interception.

Soon afterwards, when Gerrard inexplicably lost possession in midfield to the lively Perderson, the Rovers man raced on before letting fly with a booming 25-yarder which Reina, at full stretch, only just managed to push onto the crossbar. Pedersen could hardly believe his eyes – this was one almighty close shave for out-of-sorts Liverpool!

In the 39th minute, Reina was again in action, preventing his side from falling behind by diving at full length to push Pedersen's long range free-kick around a post. Liverpool responded and Gerrard tried to pick out Kuyt, but Robinson was alert to the danger and made a clean save.

As half-time approached, Rafael Benítez's side at last, were starting to dictate the pace of the game and Alonso fired in a shot from just inside the 6-yard area, which Robinson, standing tall, blocked to keep plucky Blackburn on level terms.

After a slow start to the second half, Gerrard was denied by Robinson in the 61st minute. The home 'keeper parried his well-struck shot, and as the ball broke free, the onrushing Benayoun was unable to get the right contact on the rebound. The deadlock was finally broken in the 68th minute when Gerrard delivered a cross from the right. Dutchman Kuyt took a swipe at the ball and luckily in the process of doing so, released Alonso, who beat Robinson with a rather weak low shot, which the 'keeper knew he probably should have saved! This was a worrying spell for a Blackburn side who had all but forgotten what it was like to win a league match, and they were totally deflated when Liverpool extended their lead in the 79th minute with a marvellous solo effort from Benayoun.

He latched on to an-over-the-top ball from Kuyt, skipping away from Warnock before rifling home a low shot into the corner of Robinson's net. Blackburn, nevertheless, still managed a smile and, in what transpired to be a rare attack, secured a consolation goal in the 86th minute with a smart header from Santa Cruz. The impressive Gerrard had the final word in stoppage time, however, scoring after substitute Albert Riera had laid the ball into his path with Robinson marooned.

Gerrard said after the final whistle: 'Okay, we weren't at our best, but we still won. I'll settle for playing badly and collect three points any day. Play badly a win... that's a recipe for success in anyone's language.'

31

CHAMPIONS LEAGUE, KNOCKOUT ROUND 2ND LEG
LIVERPOOL 4 REAL MADRID 0
(5-0 on aggregate)
10 March 2009

Having remained unbeaten throughout the group games, winning five (against Olympique Marseille twice, PSV Eindhoven twice and Standard Liege) and drawing three, Liverpool were strong favourites in the eyes of some bookmakers to go all the way to the final, even win the coveted trophy. And with only two defeats suffered in their twenty-eight completed Premiership matches during the season, the Reds were lying second in the table behind Manchester United and, best of all, they weren't conceding all that many goals. In contrast, Steven Gerrard, Fernando Torres and Dirk Kuyt were all in good nick and as a result the goals were going in at the right end! Ever-present Pepe Reina was in tip-top form between the posts, while Jamie Carragher was playing as well as ever at the heart of the defence.

Liverpool (4-4-2): Reina, Arbeloa, Carragher, Skrtel, Aurelio, Alonso (Lucas), Gerrard (Spearing), Mascherano, Kuyt, Torres (Dossena), Babel.
Real Madrid (4-4-2): Casillas, Ramos, Pepe, Cannavaro (Van der Vaart), Heinze, Diarra, Gago (Guti), Sneijder, Robben (Marcelo), Higuain, Raul.
Attendance: 42,550

Kevin McNamara reporting for *The Guardian*, stated:

Awe at an overwhelming victory is matched only by disbelief that Real Madrid could be so humiliated. The visitors' sole hope of explaining themselves will lie in babbling about the authority that wells up in Liverpool whenever they skip happily into this tournament. It can seem as if they don a new identity after escaping the tribulations on the domestic front. In the Champions League the blend of continental outlook and British gusto seems perfect. Juande Ramos' team were made to look a horrible concoction. Had it not been for the fact that he inherited a crisis when appointed in mid-season, the former Tottenham manager would fear dismissal today. The weakness of Real verged on the unfathomable.

On the night the Spaniards were second best in each and every department. Liverpool played with quality, conviction and honest endeavour and once had fired in the first goal, the result, in truth, was never in doubt.

Torres, although perhaps not 100 per cent fit, opened the scoring just past the quarter hour mark. In-form Gerrard doubled the lead from the penalty spot before half-time and the midfielder scored his second, and Liverpool's third, early in the second period, before substitute Dossena added a late fourth.

Leading 1-0 from the first leg (courtesy of Yossi Benayoun's 82nd minute goal in the Bernabeu), Liverpool were in the driving seat, leaving Real to do the worrying. Stevie G's men were, to a certain degree, free of any dilemma, although neutrals inside Anfield and at home would have worried whether it was worthwhile to take so many risks early on in the game by committing three or four players into attacking positions. That excellent result in the first leg had given Liverpool an enormous amount of confidence and from the start they knew, deep down, that Real were somewhat vulnerable at the back.

As early as the 4th minute, the lively Torres dragged the ball away from Pepe and tested Casillas who shortly afterwards apprehensively tipped a well struck drive from defensive midfielder Javier Mascherano over the bar. There was a brief reaction from Real as Liverpool's 'keeper Reina had to be alert to deal with Wesley Sneijder's effort from a smart cut-back by Heinze, who had got clear down the left.

An inspired Torres – playing against several of his fellow countryman of course – fired Liverpool into a deserved lead in the 16th minute. Two of Real's defenders, Pepe, and Italy's World Cup winning captain Fabio Cannavaro, were spread wide apart when Carragher hoisted a long pass downfield for Torres to chase. The striker controlled the ball superbly, found Kuyt on the right and when the Dutchman returned whipped over a cross, the Spanish striker was there to belt it beyond the despairing Iker Casillas. Real were stunned. Their passes went astray, fouls were committed frequently and two players began arguing with each other as Liverpool pressed on. In fact, the ineptness of the visitors explained why they had been dumped out of the Champions League at this stage five seasons in succession.

After dictating play 'all over the pitch' Liverpool went 2-0 ahead in the 28th minute. The referee's assistant signaled for a penalty when Xabi Alonso's pass bounced off the chest of Alvaro Arbeloa and on to the shoulder of Real left-back Gabriel Heinze, although the Argentine defender had stretched out an arm. The indignation of Heinze earned him a caution and merely delayed the penalty for almost 2 minutes, before Gerrard stepped up to convert the spot kick in style by sending Casillas the wrong way.

Everything was going Liverpool's way and with former Chelsea winger Arjen Robben seemingly carrying an injury, the Spaniards were pushed back into the own half of the field. Torres, Gerrard, Ryan Babel, and even Aurelio, all had efforts on goal as the Anfield crowd roared their favourites on. Robben did not take the field for the second half, replaced by wide man Marcelo, but before he could touch the ball, Gerrard – now seemingly uncontainable – cracked in a third goal for rampant Liverpool with a vicious half-volley after Babel had turned the Real defence inside out as he charged down the left in the 47th minute.

Rafael Benítez's side were now enjoying the lion's share of possession; indeed, during a 15-minute spell they held onto the ball for 80 per cent of the time, completing over 100 passes.

Real had simply disintegrated; Liverpool were in total control, and this enabled the boss to take off (rest really) both Man of the Match Gerrard (after 73 minutes) and Torres (84), replacing them with 20-year-old Jay Spearing and Italian Andrea Dossena respectively.

Still seeking to score more goals, it was Dossena who obliged with a fourth in the 88th minute, driving the last nail into Real's already sealed coffin. It was a truly terrific result for the Reds – a job thoroughly well done.

Liverpool were paired with Chelsea in the quarter-final and immediately Benítez said 'We didn't want that', while Stevie G admitted: 'Oh well, we would still have to meet them in the final anyway.'

NB: This disastrous 5-0 aggregate defeat was the Los Merengues' biggest in the European Cup/Champions League competition at the time.

32

PREMIER LEAGUE
MANCHESTER UNITED 1 LIVERPOOL 4
14 March 2009

Liverpool badly needed to win this encounter at Old Trafford to keep alive their hopes of challenging for the Premiership title. After a draw (with Manchester City), a defeat (at Middlesbrough) and a home win (over Sunderland) in their previous three games, they certainly didn't want their arch-rivals to collect three points and so go charging clear of the field with only ten matches remaining. Xabi Alonso was out but Fabio Aurelio, Sami Hyypiä and Fernando Torres all returned and manager Rafael Benítez was confident (as always) that his team could produce the goods.

Manchester United (4-4-2): Van der Sar, O'Shea, Ferdinand, Vidic, Evra, Ronaldo, Carrick (Giggs), Anderson (Scholes), Park (Berbatov), Rooney, Tevez.
Liverpool (4-5-1): Reina, Arbeloa, Carragher, Skrtel, Aurelio, Mascherano, Lucas, Kuyt, Gerrard (El Zhar), Riera (Dossena), Torres (Babel).
Attendance: 75,569

On a tense day in Manchester, home defender Nemanja Vidic endured a miserable afternoon as Liverpool produced terrific performance at Old Trafford to record a stunning 4-1 victory that reignited the title race. The rugged defender was badly at fault for Torres' opening goal and was sent off in the second half, his departure proving crucial to the final outcome.

Torres, who was voted Man of the Match, caused United's defence all sorts of problems. Liverpool goalkeeper Pepe Reina produced the goods to deny Carlos Tevez at a crucial time with the score at 2-1 after 75 minutes, while Andrea Dossena's late chip was absolutely brilliant and sealed a fantastic win for Liverpool. Inevitably it was Torres and the impressive Steven Gerrard who were at the hub of a victory which reduced United's lead at the top of Premier League to four points, although United did have a game in hand.

Cristiano Ronaldo's 23rd minute penalty got the home supporters cheering but the lead lasted just five minutes as Torres capitalised on Vidic's error to equalise. A minute before the interval, Gerrard picked himself up from the ground to dispatch a penalty after he had been fouled by Patrice Evra. With less than a quarter-of-an-hour remaining, Vidic saw red for a professional foul on Liverpool's skipper. From the resulting free-kick, Aurelio curled a sumptuous 25-yard effort past the crestfallen Edwin Van der Sar in the United goal.

United's woes were exacerbated in the first minute of added time when substitute Dossena lobbed in a magnificent fourth over the head of the United goalkeeper. This was Liverpool's biggest win on United soil since 1936 (when they were 5-2 victors) and it also brought them the double, having won 2-1 at Anfield in September. And they thoroughly deserved it.

Jamie Carragher was switched to right-back due to Alvaro Arbeloa's late withdrawal, and after a shaky start he settled into the game with authority. After fairly even first quarter, it was a bit of surprise when United went ahead. Reina certainly read Tevez's through pass (aimed for Park Ji-sung, well enough), but came off his line a fraction too quickly. The South Korean nicked the ball away from him, but was brought down by the 'keeper, and Staffordshire referee Alan Wiley correctly pointed to the spot.

Ronaldo duly dispatched the spot kick for his seventeenth goal of the season. Sir Alex Ferguson's men, however, failed to hold their advantage and 5 minutes later Liverpool drew level thanks to, what some people say, was a rare mistake by Vidic. The Serbian defender, who had been playing superbly all season, and was favourite to win the PFA Player of the Year award, let Martin Skrtel's long punt bounce forward when he should have headed it, and then failed to deal with the loose ball, allowing Torres to nip in, race clear, and find the net with clinical efficiency. Conceding this goal was a surprise to United's system as they had only let in two in the previous sixteen matches and although they came close to regaining the lead, they went it at half-time 2-1 down.

Torres sent Gerrard racing into the box but his run was halted by Evra's mistimed tackle, a clear penalty that the Liverpool converted with aplomb. Gerrard's glee was obvious. Liverpool's lead was fully deserved, condemning Ferguson to his first half-time rallying call in Premiership combat at Old Trafford all season.

United began the second-half with a lot more gusto, although they simply couldn't retain the ball for more than 20 seconds, Michael Carrick being the main culprit with some very wayward passes. Tevez threatened briefly, sliding a shot a yard wide, as did Ronaldo, but Liverpool's defence held firm. And as time ticked by, and with Liverpool looking solid, Ferguson took off Anderson, Park and Carrick and introduced Dimitar Berbatov, Paul Scholes and Ryan Giggs.

Nothing changed really. As United huffed and puffed, so Liverpool remained focused and any hope that Fergie's team might salvage a point evaporated within a minute of the triple substitution, when Vidic hauled down Gerrard and was banished to the dressing room.

This was, in fact, Vidic's second successive red card in games against Liverpool, and he was still making his way down the tunnel when Aurelio curled home a superb free-kick, awarded for the Serbian defender's foul on the Liverpool skipper. On a high, Liverpool came again and with time fast running out Dossena completed a memorable win with a well-judged lob. In fact, it could have been worse for United as Gerrard had earlier missed a golden chance with 5 minutes remaining, skying the ball over the top and into the Stretford End after being set up by substitute Ryan Babel. At that point the stadium was half empty, as the Liverpool fans celebrated a wonderful victory. After the game, a sorry looking Ferguson said, 'It could easily have been five or even six. They were far better than us on the day.'

Next up for Gerrard and Co. were home and away Premiership games against Aston Villa and Fulham respectively, followed by two Champions League encounters in the space of seven days against Chelsea, with a home game against Blackburn Rovers slotted in between. Things were hotting up nicely!

33

PREMIER LEAGUE
LIVERPOOL 5 ASTON VILLA 0
22 March 2009

On a high following two excellent wins – 4-0 at home against Real Madrid in the Champions League and 4-1 at Old Trafford in the Premiership – Liverpool made it thirteen goals in three games by demolishing a moderately weak Aston Villa team 5-0 with the irresistible Steven Gerrard grabbing a hat-trick. Manager Rafael Benítez was adamant before kick-off that victory was imperative against Villa. He told his players: 'You can't lose, even draw this game … if you do, then you can say goodbye to winning the Championship.'

Liverpool (4-4-2): Reina, Arbeloa (Agger), Skrtel, Carragher, Aurelio, Alonso (Lucas), Mascherano, Gerrard (N'Gog), Riera, Kuyt, Torres.
Aston Villa (3-5-2): Friedel, Cueller, Davies, L. Young, Barry, Milner, Reo-Coker (Guzan), Petrov, A. Young, Carew (Gardner), Heskey (Agbonlahor).
Attendance: 44,131

The Guardian reporter Kevin McCarra wrote, 'If high spirits could lift a side to the peak of the Premier League then it would be Liverpool's destiny to take the title.' After this excellent victory over Villa, Rafael Benítez's team moved to within a point of table-toppers Manchester United who had a game in hand, but Liverpool were now in full flow and looked in supreme form.

At a meeting following the game, a calm-faced Benítez complained that his players should have scored more goals. 'Forget five, it should have been six, seven, even eight', he said. 'But we won – that was what we had to do, so why moan. We are still in with a chance of becoming champions.'

Villa, managed by former Northern Ireland international Martin O'Neill, were lying fifth in the table before kick-off. However, they hadn't won in eight games in all competitions, and by all accounts had been performing rather poorly since beating Blackburn in early February.

Form rarely lies; in fact, it was spot on this time, as the Midlanders struggled for long periods and despite the odd counter-attack, were always under the cosh –

more so after their American goalkeeper Brad Friedel had been shown a red card halfway through the second half. Liverpool, it must be said, were full of gusto and commitment, and effectively they controlled the game from the very first whistle.

Before the match kicked off, everyone inside Anfield obeyed a minute's silence in honour of club secretary Bryce Morrison who had recently passed away, but once that ceremony was over it was Liverpool who took control. In the end, it was Man of the Match Steven Gerrard, with the aid of two penalties, who stole the show, as he notched the first league hat-trick of his professional career.

Villa were no match for Liverpool. O'Neill's team struggled to string two or three passes together and managed only a handful of worthwhile attacks in the entire ninety-odd minutes. Admittedly, Villa were without reliable centre-back and club captain Martin Laursen, who damaged his knee in December, but they were outclassed in every department, which was surprising as they had already won ten away games during the season, including victories at Arsenal, Everton and Tottenham.

With barely 8 minutes gone, Liverpool deservedly took the lead. Gerrard's whipping free-kick was headed against the bar by Spanish midfielder Xabi Alonso, and with the visitors' defence all at sea, alert Dutchman Dirk Kuyt pounced to drill home the loose ball. Then, out of the blue was a pivotal incident that could well have tipped the game in a more conventional direction (we'll never know really). Villa's tall Norwegian striker John Carew got on the end of Ashley Young's measured cross. He connected well enough with the ball but Liverpool's 'keeper Pepe Reina somehow got up to claw his powerful header away from the top corner of his goal at the expense of a flag kick.

Liverpool hit back strongly and after a couple of near misses, went 2-0 up in the 33rd minute. Reina was well positioned to save a Gareth Barry free-kick and from his long downfield clearance, the bouncing ball was collected by Albert Riera and, with covering defender Luke Young unable to intervene, the Spanish forward took aim before firing hard and low past Friedel.

Liverpool were now purring and, after Kuyt and Torres had almost broken through again, 2-0 became 3-0 6 minutes before half-time. Villa's energetic midfielder Nigel Reo-Coker overcommitted himself and clearly fouled Riera inside the area. Penalty said the referee, and up stepped Gerrard to slot home the first of his two 12-yard kicks.

Villa were all but helpless at this juncture and could hardly muster a worthwhile attack. It then got worse for the visitors 5 minutes after the interval, when Stevie G, the impressive Liverpool captain, struck again in clinical fashion after Alonso had tapped a free-kick to him. Super Steven then banged home his second spot kick of the game in the 65th minute following a foul where Friedel floored Fernando Torres as the Spaniard skipped round him.

At the time, the question was asked as to whether or not there had been any element of intent by the USA No. 1, but it would also have been totally wrong if referee Martin Atkinson had let play continue with a goal there for the taking (or scoring)! Off went the unfortunate Friedel to be replaced by fellow countryman Brad Guzan, who was making his Premier League debut. He got nowhere near Gerrard's second penalty as Liverpool roared into a five-goal lead. And in fact it was their second nap hand of the season, having won 5-1 at Newcastle in late December, when Gerrard netted twice.

With a quarter of the game still remaining, Liverpool went for the kill, but they simply couldn't force the ball into the Villa net – Torres, Kuyt, Gerrard and substitute David N'Gog all going close. To give Guzan some credit, he did pull off three excellent saves.

Barry, whom Liverpool had tried to sign at one stage, tried his best to get Villa going, but he was overpowered in midfield. Annoying, the Reds couldn't add to their goal tally despite being on top.

In the end, it turned out to be a very comfortable and indeed one-sided victory, but realistically Liverpool had to win all of their remaining eight Premiership matches to stand any chance of pipping their arch-rivals Manchester United to the title. A tall order in anyone's language – even Steven Gerrard's!

NB: *In this game, Liverpool's goalkeeper Pepe Reina kept his 100th clean sheet for the club.*

34

CHAMPIONS LEAGUE, QUARTER-FINAL 2ND LEG
CHELSEA 4 LIVERPOOL 4
(7-5 on aggregate)
14 April 2009

I've included this game in my top fifty, although Steven Gerrard didn't take part in it. He was sidelined through injury but was there on the sidelines roaring his side on, and one feels that if he had been out there under the floodlights, Liverpool could well have won.

Having lost their home leg 3-1, Liverpool knew they had to score at least twice at Stamford Bridge to reach the semi-finals of the Champions League. It was a big ask, a tall order, but manager Rafael Benítez said, 'We can do it. There's no doubt about that, my players will be up for a fight. We will be in attack mode and we'll give it a real go.' Chelsea lined up without their influential skipper and centre-back John Terry.

Chelsea (4-2-3-1): Čech, Ivanovic, Alex, Carvalho, Ashley Cole, Kalou (Anelka), Ballack, Essien, Lampard, Malouda, Drogba (Di Santo).
Liverpool (4-4-1-1): Reina, Arbeloa (Babel), Carragher, Skrtel, Aurelio, Lucas, Mascherano (Riera), Alonso, Kuyt, Benayoun, Torres (N'Gog).
Attendance: 38,286

This was without doubt a cracking encounter, action packed from start to finish, and the final result could easily have been 6-6, 8-8 even 10-10. And in the end it was gallant Liverpool who were the desperately unlucky losers despite scoring five goals, four away from home. Chelsea had already survived a massive scare by drawing one of the most entertaining Champions League games of recent times before sealing a 7-5 aggregate win to clinch a semi-final clash with Barcelona.

Guus Hiddink's team saw their two-goal lead from the Anfield leg blown away by Fabio Aurelio's free-kick and a penalty from Xabi Alonso before half-time. In the space of 6 dramatic second-half minutes, a horrid mistake by Liverpool 'keeper José Reina, who conceded an own goal from Didier Drogba's flick and a thunderbolt free-kick from centre-back Alex, brought the scores level.

Frank Lampard then put Chelsea 3-2 ahead on the night, before Lucas Leiva's deflected strike and a near-post header from Dirk Kuyt sent Liverpool in front at 4-3. It was brilliant stuff.

The Stamford Bridge faithful were stunned, knowing that the Reds required just one more goal to complete a sensational victory on away goals ... and there were 7 minutes plus added time to come! Unfortunately for Liverpool, that man Lampard pounced again to bring the scores level and so end what had been a truly memorable game of football.

Liverpool, without their inspirational skipper Stevie G, came so close to pulling off one of the greatest and indeed memorable victories in the club's history. The Reds gave the hosts an early warning when a superb touch from Yossi Benayoun on 13 minutes created a clear opening for Fernando Torres, but the Spaniard failed to hit the target with his left-foot strike. It was a bad miss and Liverpool's initially slim hopes were almost completely extinguished 50 seconds later when Lampard missed the target by inches with a scrumptious free-kick.

Soon afterwards there came a moment that home goalkeeper Petr Čech will never forget. He asked for only one player to stand in the defensive wall to cover a free-kick, but put his hands on his head when full-back Fabio Aurelio sent the ball scurrying past him and into the bottom corner of his net on 19 minutes. Čech had anticipated dealing with a floated ball into the congested area but was caught completely out of position as Aurelio's kick went in.

Buoyed by their goal, Liverpool suddenly put some extra bite and rhythm into their play while Chelsea looked uncharacteristically brittle at the back. Indeed, the home defensive unit struggled at times to cope with the swift passing and quick movement of the Liverpool players, who had struggled so badly at Anfield eight days earlier.

It came as no surprise when the visitors doubled their lead in the 28th minute. Alonso's hit an unstoppable penalty after the Spaniard had been fouled by Chelsea's first-leg hero Branislav Ivanovic. Chelsea boss Hiddink immediately withdrew Salomon Kalou and brought on striker Nicolas Anelka after 35 minutes. His bold decision paid dividends 7 minutes after the restart when his low cross from the right was deflected by Drogba towards Reina, who could only parry the ball into his own net. 3 minutes later, the lively Drogba was only inches away with a free-kick, but another dead-ball situation in the 57th minute brought an equaliser, with Brazilian defender Alex drilling home a long-range effort with immense power.

As it stood, Liverpool now needed to score twice more and hold out to win the tie on aggregate. It was going to be tough. Realistically Michael Ballack – after being set up by Drogba – should have put the result beyond doubt, but he shot tamely, allowing Reina to save comfortably to his right.

Torres, an increasingly marginal figure, went close from distance as Liverpool came again, but it was Chelsea who were in control at this juncture and with a quarter of an hour remaining Lampard put his team ahead at 3-2 with a close-range finish from another precise Drogba cross.

The tie seemed to be dead and buried, but Liverpool still had something left in the tank and when Lucas saw his shot deflected in on 81 minutes; Stevie G was on his feet just 55 seconds later when Kuyt produced a bullet header from substitute Albert Riera's cross to edge the visitors back in front at 4-3. It was tense, mighty tense.

Suddenly it was Liverpool supporters who were in full voice – you could hear them in Central London – but their cheers and encouragement crumbled when the final goal of a pulsating match was scored in the 89th minute by Lampard with a low drive which flew in after striking both posts.

There was hardly any time remaining for Liverpool to respond, but the fragile Čech still managed to fumble a cross that substitute David N'Gog drilled towards goal, forcing a superb headed clearance from Michael Essien. When Spanish referee Luis Medina Cantalejo blew the final whistle it was Chelsea who celebrated while Liverpool trooped off the field, heads bowed and looking rather downhearted after a truly great battle.

35

INTERNATIONAL WORLD CUP QUALIFIER
ENGLAND 5 CROATIA 1
9 September 2009

A draw in this game would have been enough to secure England's place in the 2010 World Cup finals following Ukraine's goalless match in Belarus, but Fabio Capello's men didn't want to play for a draw, they wanted to thrash Croatia and so rub salt into the wounds of their opponents whom they had flattened 4-1 in Zagreb twelve months earlier.

With the fixture taking place on the 9th day of the 9th month of the 9th year of the twenty-first century, one felt that England simply wanted to make it another 'nine' in terms of goals scored over the two games against Croatia, who crucially were missing several key players – the headline absentee being Luka Modric of Tottenham, who was out with a broken leg.

The only change made by Capello (from the side that had defeated Slovenia in a friendly a few days earlier) was Aaron Lennon, who was selected on the right side of midfield in place of the ineffective Shaun Wright-Phillips. However, the England chief resisted the temptation to alter his frontline with Emile Heskey again being preferred to the in-form Jermain Defoe, who was named as one of the substitutes. For Steven Gerrard it was to be his seventy-sixth senior appearance for his country.

England (4-4-2): Green, Johnson, Terry, Upson, A. Cole, Lennon (Beckham), Barry, Lampard, Gerrard (Milner), Rooney, Heskey (Defoe).
Croatia (4-4-2): Runje, Srna, Krizanac, Simunic, Pranji, Mandzukic, Vukojevic, Pokrivac (Ratitic), Kranjcar, Eduardo (Klasnic), Olic (Petric).
Attendance: 87,319

All the pre-match questions as to whether or not England would qualify for the 2010 World Cup in South Africa were answered quite emphatically when they produced a terrific performance at Wembley. From the very first whistle England were on the ball, pressing the Croatians back deep into their own half of the field. All ten outfield players were fired up, full of determination and running, and after just 7 minutes they were ahead.

The pace of the Tottenham winger Aaron Lennon had already scared the Croatians and when he threatened again, by cutting across the face of the goal from a yard or so inside the penalty area, a clumsy challenge from Josip Simonic gave Spanish referee Alberto Ubdiano Mallenco no option but to award a spot kick. Up stepped the ever reliable Frank Lampard to find the net with an exact replica of his penalty against Slovenia four days earlier. This was just the start England wanted, and they went in search of more goals, never taking the foot off the accelerator for a minute. They completely dominated proceedings and may well have bagged another five or six goals before half-time.

Soon after the opening goal, Steven Gerrard headed a Wayne Rooney cross over the top and Gareth Barry saw a screamer saved by the diving Vedran Runje to his right. Then, on 17 minutes, Gerrard's measured pass found Lennon out on the right and his precise cross to the far post was met full on by the incoming Liverpool captain who netted with a glorious header to make it 2-0.

The opening 20 minutes had been superb for England. The bemused Croatians did come into the game briefly, after falling two behind – Nico Kranjcar (soon to join Spurs and later QPR) having their best chance (off target) – but Capello's men always looked in control.

Barry was playing superbly with Gerrard in midfield, who was intercepting, making good tackles, supporting the attack and always ensuring he was available to take the pressure of his defenders. Croatia, in fact, looked poor and hardly troubled goalkeeper Rob Green, whose only activity was to clear three back passes and collect two high looping crosses.

In the 27th minute, Lampard saw his 35-yard free-kick clawed away by Runje; Rooney cleverly put Lennon clear but the goalkeeper was there again to divert the danger and if Emile Heskey's first touch had been better he surely would have scored following another purposeful attack.

Croatia simply had no answer to England's overall dominance. It was terrific stuff and the crowd loved it. On 38 minutes the impressive Gerrard had another chance down the left as he broke clear. He knew he should have finished better. Still, the chances kept coming and 3 minutes before the interval, Heskey took his eye off the ball believing he was offside, which he wasn't, and a golden chance went begging. 60 seconds later, Heskey set up Lampard, but the Chelsea man completely fluffed his shot when well placed. Just before the break, Lampard returned the compliment by setting up Heskey, but again the big forward missed a rather simple chance. As they left the field for a deserved cuppa, the England players were given a standing ovation by the Wembley crowd, and rightly so.

Croatia brought on two substitutes at the start of the second half and for 10 minutes they look much better, retaining possession well and making England work a lot harder than at any time in the match. However, England quickly got back on track and in the 58th minutes scored a third goal, and what a stunning effort it was. Lennon was again involved, passing to Gerrard who, in turn, found Glen Johnson down the right wing. Some tricky footwork ensured from the right-back, and his wonderful cross was met by Lampard whose deft header found the bottom of Runje's net.

8 minutes later it was 4-0 as Gerrard, Barry and Rooney combined for the latter to cross into the middle where the Liverpool star, free once again, scored with another well directed header.

Ironic cheers were heard in the 69th minute when Croatia had their first shot on target, but Kranjcar's effort was saved comfortably by Green. But just as England were congratulating themselves on a tight defensive performance, they conceded a goal. Johnson, who was playing very well at right-back, was turned far too easily by Croatian wide man Mladan Petric and the Croat's cross, Green made a fabulous diving save to his left to keep out Eduardo's header. However, the ball spun loose and although the 'keeper saved well again, this time from Mario Mandzukic, Eduardo was there in the right position at the right time to whip the second rebound into the net. If Green was annoyed, you should have seen Capello's reaction! He was furious!

That blip, thankfully, was quickly forgiven as England went down the field to make it 5-1 on 76 minutes. This time it was impressive Croatian goalkeeper Runje who gifted the home side a goal. He tried to kick clear a back-pass and only succeeded in slicing his clearance straight to Rooney, who had the easiest of tasks to score his ninth goal of the campaign. It was a shame for Runje who prior to that had produced two or three brilliant saves, as well as doing his fair share of blocking.

There is no doubt whatsoever that England thoroughly deserved to win. They produced a sparkling all-round team performance, the best seen at Wembley for many a year. It was truly a great night. Gerrard, Lampard, Barry and Rooney were all outstanding, and although the World Cup itself was still some way off, confidence in the camp was high.

NB: Rooney's goal brought his tally to eight in a World Cup qualifying campaign, beating the previous record of seven set by Tommy Taylor, who died in the Munich air crash before the 1958 World Cup was played.

36

EUROPA LEAGUE SEMI-FINAL 2ND LEG
LIVERPOOL 2 ATLÉTICO MADRID 1
(2-2 on aggregate; Reds lost on away goal rule)
29 April 2010

After losing 1-0 in the first leg of this Europa League semi-final at the Vicente Calderon Stadium in Spain – Diego Forlan scoring the vital 9th minute goal – Liverpool manager Rafael Benítez talked at length about his side's chances in the return fixture at Anfield, revealing that one of his backroom team hallucinated that Liverpool would win 3-1 and go forward 3-2 on aggregate.

'I was talking with our laundry man leaving Melwood', he told reporter Barry Glendenning of The Guardian. *'I think about the Olympiakos game (in 2005). We will score at the end and win 3-1 against Atlético', said Benítez. 'The people have the belief, the staff have the belief and the players have the belief.' That was it; it would be Liverpool against Fulham or Hamburg in the final.*

Liverpool striker Dirk Kuyt was declared fit to play after recovering from a calf injury, but Benítez still made two changes from the side that beat Burnley 4-0 the previous Sunday. Defensive midfielder Javier Mascherano was switched to right-back, allowing Glen Johnson to move to the left; the Brazilian Lucas returned to play alongside Steven Gerrard in central midfield; Daniel Ayala dropped to the bench; and Yossi Benayoun came into the side on the right for the ineligible Maxi Rodriguez. Atletico made three changes from the first leg, the most significant being the return of striker Sergio Aguero after suspension. Aguero, of course, joined Manchester City in 2011.

Liverpool (4-4-2): Reina, Mascherano (Degen), Carragher, Agger, Johnson, Gerrard, Lucas, Benayoun (Pacheco), Aquilani (El Zhar), Babel, Kuyt.
Atlético Madrid (4-4-2): De Gea, Valera, Dominguez, Perea, Antonio Lopez, Reyes, Paulo Assuncao (Jurado), Raul Garcia, Simao, Aguero (Salvio), Forlan (Camacho).
Attendance: 42,040.

Agonisingly for the Liverpool faithful, players, management, supporters alike, ex-Manchester United forward Diego Forlan came back (again) to haunt the Reds with a dramatic late strike that booked his side a place in the final on the away goal rule.

Liverpool deservedly drew level on aggregate after Alberto Aquilani's 44th minute effort and they certainly had the better of the exchanges in the second half as the game went into extra time. When Yossi Benayoun grabbed a 95th minute overall lead, it looked as though the Reds had reached another major cup final. But what a shock they got!

The Uruguayan Forlan, who was much derided during his time in English football, had the last word when he struck a decisive and cruel blow in the 102nd minute to put an end to the Merseyside team's involvement in the competition. Liverpool needed to get out of the traps quickly, which they almost got after barely ten seconds. Daniel Agger's long ball was collected by Benayoun inside Atlético's penalty area, but his low drive, albeit from a narrow angle, was turned aside by future Old Trafford goalkeeper David de Gea, who then had an easier save to make when Aquilani shot straight at him in the 11th minute.

It was obvious from the word go that Atlético's game plan was to sit back and counter-attack when possible, with Forlan their main outlet on the left. But with the nippy Aguero not too far away from him, the duo still posed an occasional threat and Liverpool's keeper Pepe Reina had to dive low to his right to turn Raul Garcia's long-range effort around the post midway through the first half. Liverpool still had to push forward and Kuyt's effort flew only inches over the top after the Dutchman had slid into the 6-yard box to get a touch on Javier Mascherano's low, tempting cross.

At this juncture, the game was more far more open than expected and Liverpool's defenders at times had to be on their guard. They had a lucky escape on 25 minutes when Aguero skipped round Reina from Jose Antonio Reyes' perfect through-ball. Fortunately, the impish Argentine opted to cross rather than shoot from a narrow angle and Forlan, charging in, could not make up the ground in time.

Liverpool thought they had made the breakthrough they wanted in the 32nd minute when Steven Gerrard curled in a free-kick into the danger zone and onto the head of Agger, whose effort found the bottom corner of De Gea's net only for an offside flag to rule the goal out. Gerrard was then booked for a needless foul on Aguero as half-time approached, but then, when least expected and with just seconds to go before the interval, Liverpool scored and the goal came with one of the simplest moves possible!

Stand-in right-back Mascherano's quick throw was collected by Benayoun, who had drifted out to the wing. He was allowed to whip in a cross that was completely missed by Kuyt but found Aquilani instead, allowing the Italian to curl home a low shot just inside De Gea's left-hand post. Anfield erupted; the tie was all square.

With honours even, Liverpool's approach play was more precise as the second half began, but the atmosphere inside the ground, as expected, was still tense, and the players could feel it as Benayoun smashed an effort well over from 25 yards. Roared on by the Kop, Liverpool somehow managed to find an extra gear and when Johnson cut in from the left and whipped in a right-footed shot, De Gea could only parry the ball over his own crossbar. The resulting corner however, swung over by Stevie G, was easily collected by the goalkeeper.

After precious few chances had been created, the last 10 minutes of normal time saw Atlético have by far their best spell of the game, but first Aguero and then Forlan mis-controlled the ball inside the penalty area with the home defence backing off, while the last chance of the second half drifted away when Liverpool successfully applied the offside trap..

Knowing that if Atlético scored they would surely win, it was now crucial that Liverpool took the initiative and 5 minutes into the extra-time period they went ahead for the first time. Shear joy on the Kop. Gerrard's teasing free-kick was only half cleared and as the ball came out of the crowded penalty area Lucas lobbed it back into the inside-left channel, where Benayoun, played onside by the slow-moving Antonio Lopez, smashed in a smart left-footer. De Gea got a hand to it but couldn't prevent it from crossing the line.

Atlético's substitute José Manuel Jurado then fired in 20-yard drive, which flew just inches wide of Reina's post. This was a warning to Liverpool who fell to a killer punch in the 102nd minute.

Reyes beat Johnson on the left flank and delivered a cross to the unmarked Forlan, who stabbed home from close range with Liverpool defenders Agger and Carragher starring at each other.

This was a body blow. Liverpool knew they had to score again and quickly, or they would be out (beaten by an away goal). But for all their endeavour and determination in the second period of extra time, it was not to be. In fact, Simao Sabrosa almost earned the Spanish club a draw on the night when his booming drive flew inches over Reina's crossbar.

Liverpool's European dreams, and their hopes of a successful conclusion to their drab season, were extinguished. It was a sad night at Anfield, summed up by a disappointed Stevie G who said, 'We simply didn't perform. We were certainly up for it and I thought we had won it with Yossi's goal, but all credit to Atlético. They played the right sort of game.'

NB: For the record, Atlético beat Fulham 2-1 after extra time in the final, which took place in Hamburg.

37

INTERNATIONAL FRIENDLY
ENGLAND 2 HUNGARY 1
11 August 2010

Head coach Fabio Capello hinted some days earlier that he would make 'many changes' to his team for this friendly against the 60th ranked country in world football – Hungary. And he also stated publicly that Steven Gerrard would wear the captain's armband for the first time at senior level.

In his squad Capello named seven uncapped players: twenty-two-year-old goalkeepers Frankie Fielding (Derby County), and Scott Loach (Ipswich Town); left-back Kieran Gibbs (Arsenal); central defenders Gary Cahill (Bolton Wanderers) and Matthew Dawson (Spurs); midfielder Jack Wilshire (Arsenal); and striker Bobby Zamora (Fulham).

England (4-2-3-1): Hart, G. Johnson, Jagielka, Terry (Dawson), A. Cole (Gibbs), Gerrard (Wilshere), Barry, Walcott (A. Young), Lampard (Zamora), A. Johnson, Rooney (Milner).
Hungary (4-4-2): Kiraly, Sliptak (Komlosi), Vanczak (Zsolt), Juhasz, Szelesi, Vadocz, Dzudzsak (Koman), Gergeley, Elek (Toth), Gera, Huszti (Priskin).
Attendance: 72,034

I will be truthful – Capello's 'new' England team produced a very good performance against a workmanlike Hungarian side. All the pre-match media talk, which hinted that the players would receive a 'rough reception' from the Wembley faithful following a very disappointing World Cup, didn't materialize, and in fact when the teams took the field there was more cheering and clapping than there were boos and jeers.

The hard-done-by fans took time to see how things would transpire out on the pitch, but they quickly warmed to the effort, showing determination and skill during the first half. It got better, to a certain extent, after the interval as England went on to record a well-deserved victory, albeit by a rather narrow margin. The younger players involved in the action could certainly hold their heads up high.

Right from the first whistle, sounded by French referee Stéphane Lannoy, England zipped the ball around at a quick tempo with four and sometimes five players pressing forward at will. Wayne Rooney had the ball in the net as early as the 2nd minute but his effort was clearly offside, and on 12 minutes Frank Lampard sent the ball into space with a ballooning drive – a horrible miss.

Wide man Adam Johnson and Theo Walcott looked sharp with their nimble footwork that had the crowd buzzing, but unfortunately the final ball into the danger zone was often disappointing. Rooney, who looked as if he was not fully enjoying the role as a lone forward, had the first effort on goal, shooting weakly from distance. He also cleverly brought his colleagues into play with some astute passes. Phil Jagielka, who it must be said had an excellent game and had England's first goal chance early on, could only poke the ball wide of the target following a corner kick.

England dominated the first quarter of an hour and it seemed inevitable that a goal would arrive but some determined defending by the visitors kept Gerrard and Co. at bay. England should have opened the scoring in the 20th minute. A swift-flowing move down the right involving Gerrard, Glen Johnson and Walcott ended with the latter pulling the ball across the face of Gabor Kiraly's goal and into the path of Adam Johnson. But possibly the excitement of the occasion got to the Manchester City forward, who somehow saw his close-range shot fly over the top when it seemed easier to score.

At the other end of the field, Johnson's clubmate, Joe Hart, making his first start in goal, pulled off a good save from Akos Elek and went on to produce a fine display, being positive in everything he did, especially in his handling of high crosses, although these were few and far between. 'He's here to stay', said one reporter.

England's back four, with John Terry in the thick of things when it had to be, all played well and were never in any serious trouble during a one-sided first half. The only criticism fired at England revolved around their overall attacking play. Rooney, it seemed, spent far too much time in his own half of the field, playing nearer the penalty area than the halfway line, and when the wingers gained possession, they had to hold up play and pass backwards.

Frank Lampard and Gareth Barry played far deeper than normal and it worked, giving skipper Stevie G time and space to support the Manchester United player when he could get forward! Unfortunately, clear-cut chances were few and far between during the second part of the of the opening half. Only Gerrard's free-kick on the half hour mark came close, which was tipped over by goalkeeper Kiraly, along with a shot from the Liverpool dynamo that was saved in the 33rd minute.

Although there was some spasmodic booing as the teams walked off at the break, the majority of the large crowd had witnessed some good passages of play and things looked promising.

At the start of the second period, Capello brought on three debutants – Gibbs for Ashley Cole, Zamora for Lampard and Dawson for Terry. Ashley Young also came on for Walcott, and straightaway all four players were involved in the action as England began at a brisk pace.

Young whipped over a terrific cross from the left, after linking up with Gibbs, and two threatening through balls by Gerrard and Barry, almost divided the entire Hungarian defence.

The last thing England needed at this stage was to concede a goal and amazingly that's what happened. In the 62nd minute, having had over 65 per cent of the play, a direct through ball was completely missed by Dawson, allowing Fulham's Zoltan Gera to break clear. He picked out Szaboics Huszti on his left and, when his low cross came flying towards the danger zone, he managed to get a touch on the ball, sending it beyond a despairing Joe Hart. Dawson had done well to get back but he failed to hook the ball away to safety. Between them, the French linesman and referee decided that the ball had definitely crossed the line and awarded a goal.

This was ironic, considering that a few weeks earlier, Frank Lampard's 'goal' against Germany in England's World Cup encounter in South Africa was not given. This time at Wembley in a non-competitive match, replays afterwards clearly indicated that Dawson had managed to prevent the ball from crossing the goalline.

Thankfully, to their eternal credit, England knuckled down to business. The tempo of the game increased tenfold and deservedly their efforts were rewarded. It was captain courageous Gerrard who turned the game around. On 69 minutes he delivered a measured pass to Gibbs, but when the full-back's movement was blocked, the Liverpool midfielder latched on to the rebound, strode forward a yard or so and hit an unstoppable 35-yard right foot bullet past the goalkeeper from the edge of the area. It was a magnificent strike – his eighteenth for his country – and brought England a thoroughly deserved equaliser.

It lifted the crowd, and 4 minutes later the stadium crowd went wild as Young got his pass through to Gerrard, who was standing with his back to goal, a yard or so inside the box. With some superb footwork, the Liverpool star tricked his way round two players in a relatively short space, before flicking the ball wide of the despairing 'keeper Kiraly. Another terrific goal.

Substitute Zamora came mighty close to adding a third goal with a rasping drive that was tipped over as England ended the match on a high. But, as they say, it's not over until the final whistle sounds. With only seconds remaining, Gera combined with Tamas Priskin and with only Hart to beat, the Hungarian hesitated and saw his effort blocked by the advancing 'keeper. It was a close call, but England deserved to win, having had 62.3 per cent of the play, fourteen attempts on goal and forced fourteen corners.

After tasting victory in his first game as England captain, Stevie G said: 'To see the team giving everything is all that the crowd really wanted. Not one of the players could be faulted for their efforts. There was a lot to be pleased about, not least by the mature performances produced by the youngsters.' 'The crowd went home very 'appy', said a delighted Fabio Mr Capello, who added, 'We want a repeat performance against Bulgaria next month in a game that really matters.'

38

INTERNATIONAL EUROPEAN CHAMPIONSHIP QUALIFIER
ENGLAND 4 BULGARIA 0
3 September 2010

England boss Fabio Capello knew, as did the fans and also the players, that victory in their first European Championship qualifier against Bulgaria was imperative. 'This is one game we have to win; nothing else will do', said the Italian. After beating Hungary in what was technically a warm-up friendly, he was confident of success.

Also in Group G were Montenegro, Switzerland and Wales and the realists associated with England clearly believed that a maximum tally of 24 points could be achieved ... and why not!

The Chelsea duo of Frank Lampard (groin) and John Terry (hamstring) were ruled out, allowing Phil Jagielka to slot into the centre of the defence alongside Matthew Upson.

In-form Arsenal winger Theo Walcott was chosen on the right flank. with James Milner switching inside to accompany Gareth Barry and captain Steven Gerrard in the engine room.

Capello admitted on the eve of the match that he knew who ten members of the starting XI would be, and news soon leaked that Jermain Defoe would get the nod to partner Wayne Rooney up front. Joe Hart, England's third-choice goalkeeper at the World Cup, was now No. 1, due no doubt both to Robert Green's error against the USA and David James' age.

Bulgaria were without their most famous star, Dimitar Berbatov, ex-Manchester United of course, who had retired from international football. Aston Villa's midfielder Stiliyan Petrov and his brother Martin (Bolton) were two of their key players, along with the former Manchester City striker Valeri Bojinov.

England (4-4-2): Hart, G. Johnson, Jagielka, Dawson (Cahill), A. Cole, Walcott (A. Johnson), Gerrard, Barry, Milner, Defoe (Young), Rooney.
Bulgaria (4-4-1-1): Mihailov, Ivanov, Milanov, Manolev (Minev), Iliyan Stoyanov, Yankov, Angelov, S. Petrov, M. Petrov, Bojinov (Rangelov), Popov (Peev).
Attendance: 73,246.

There was a good-sized crowd inside Wembley when referee Viktor Kassai of Hungary set the ball rolling, and from the very first whistle England were on the front foot. After a couple of determined attacks led by Stevie G, it was the lively Defoe who established the foundations with a 3rd minute goal to ease any concerns that the home supporters had! Rooney's brilliant pass found Ashley Cole and when the attacking full-back pulled the ball across the 6-yard box, Defoe was there to volley it with venom high into the net, well beyond the reach of Bulgaria 'keeper Nikolay Mihailov.

Gerrard was relishing his central midfield role, dictating the tempo of the game and showing his full range of passing as England completely dominated the early exchanges, but Bulgaria were almost handed a route back into the game from the unlikeliest of sources. Glen Johnson lost his bearings as he attempted to deal with a cross, but thankfully, as the ball flew towards goal, an instinctive save from the alert Hart kept England ahead.

England continued to run the show and Gerrard, Defoe, Rooney and Walcott all had chances to increase the lead, but as Capello and his players went into the dressing room at half-time, they knew the game was still in the balance!

Like it was the start of the game, England burst out on the traps for the second half and in the 49th minute Rooney demonstrated his enduring quality with a clever 20-yard chip that forced Mihailov into a scrambling over the top save.

Bulgaria responded and Iselin Popov flashed a shot across the face of Hart's goal before England were forced into a substitution following Dawson's unfortunate departure through injury, with Bolton's Gary Cahill coming on for his international debut. He settled in quickly and after one important tackle, two decisive moments just after the hour saw the game swing decisively in England's favour.

Hart did well to block a powerful drive from Stanislav Angelov and as defence quickly changed to attack, Gerrard and Rooney combined to set up Defoe for another clinical finish on 61 minutes. Hart then came to England's rescue again with a superb one-handed save from Dimitar Rangelov, as the Bulgars hit back.

Walcott, who had been a peripheral figure, was replaced by Adam Johnson as the clock slowly ticked down and almost immediately Gerrard came mightily close to grabbing a third goal, but was denied by the impressive Mihailov who dived low to save his shot and then recovered well to claw away a loose ball with Defoe ready to pounce.

Substitute Johnson had proved a lively introduction and he got on the scoresheet for the first time at senior international level with a low drive that seemed to catch Mihailov unawares. With England totally in charge, it was left to Defoe to round things off in the 86th minute. He completed his hat-trick after more good work by Rooney by smashing the ball home in style, although he picked up a knock for his efforts and limped off to loud applause from the crowd.

Although the suffering home fans witnessed the occasional anxious moment and saw goalkeeper Joe Hart produce some crucial saves, there were plenty of positives, with Gerrard, Barry and Rooney all producing excellent performances.

Next up for Capello's men was a trip to Switzerland. The manager declared: 'This will be a much sterner test in Basle, but this result against Bulgaria is the perfect tonic after the trauma of South Africa.' As it was, England beat the Swiss 3-1 (Rooney, Darren Bent and Adam Johnson the scorers), and went on to qualify comfortably for Euro' 2012 as unbeaten Group G winners with 18 points. However, in Ukraine and Russia, after winning their group (just), England succumbed 4-2 on penalties to Italy (after a 0-0 draw) in the first knockout round. Once again there were plenty of sorry looking faces both on and off the pitch!

39

LEAGUE CUP FINAL
CARDIFF CITY 2 LIVERPOOL 2
(Reds won 3-2 on penalties)
26 February 2012

Liverpool last won a major domestic trophy in 2006 when they lifted the FA Cup against West Ham United. Their last appearance in a League Cup final was a year earlier (2005), when they were beaten by Chelsea. Their previous victory in a League Cup final, however, was in 2003, when they defeated Manchester United.

This Wembley encounter against Championship side Cardiff City was, in effect, a banana-skin match in which the underdogs had nothing to lose. Indeed, Liverpool manager Kenny Dalglish was apprehensive before kick-off, saying, 'You take nothing for granted in football ... anything can happen. There have been upsets before and there will be plenty more upsets in years to come. Let's hope there's not one today!'

Liverpool's first of seven League Cup final victories came in 1981. Others followed in 1982, 1983, 1984, 1995, 2001 and 2003. Cardiff had lost in the 2008 FA Cup final but this was to be their first ever appearance in a League Cup final, and they were rank outsiders according to the bookies.

On their way to reaching this final, Liverpool had eliminated Exeter City, Brighton & Hove Albion, Stoke City and Chelsea all away from home, and Manchester City 3-2 on aggregate in the semi-final. Cardiff meanwhile, had knocked out Oxford United, Huddersfield Town, Leicester City, Burnley, Blackburn Rovers and Crystal Palace, and Steven Gerrard's cousin, Anthony, was set to be named in their squad. He had made 163 League appearances for Walsall before joining the Bluebirds in 2009. but it would be a heartbreak afternoon for the tall defender.

The Welsh outsiders, lying fourth in the Championship, had been hugely impressive during the first two-thirds of the season, with Don Cowie, Icelandic international Aron Gunnarsson and Peter Whittingham their stand-out players. Manager Malky Mackay – who had steered both Norwich City and West Ham to promotion – had done sterling work in fashioning a new and resourceful team, and was confident that his players would give Liverpool a run for their money ... and so it proved!

Cardiff City (4-4-2): Heaton, McNaughton (Blake), Taylor, Gunnarson, Hudson (Gerrard), Tuner, Cowie, Whittingham, Miller, Gestede, Mason (King).
Liverpool (4-3-1-2): Reina, Johnson, Skrtel, Agger (Carragher), Enrique, Adam, Henderson (Bellamy), Gerrard, Downing, Suarez, Carroll (Kuyt).
Attendance: 89,044

Liverpool certainly started confidently enough and right-back Glen Johnson struck Tom Heaton's woodwork in the game's first meaningful attack. Steven Gerrard then surged forward from his own half to feed Johnson, who bent his shot over Heaton but saw the ball bounce back into play off the underside of the bar. Gerrard unfortunately fired the rebound over.

Cardiff hung in there gallantly, but with Stewart Downing and Jordan Henderson seeing plenty of the ball, Liverpool started to dominate and managed to get in crosses aimed at striker Andy Carroll. There was no end product to Liverpool's attacks and the Bluebirds began to get a foothold in the game.

They had already threatened through Scottish striker Kenny Miller, who blasted over from the edge of the box before the lively Joe Mason put them ahead in the 18th minute. A poor defensive header by Martin Skrtel was collected by Kevin McNaughton, whose pass found the unmarked Miller who set Mason free to power home a vicious, low shot under Pepe Reina as he rushed off his line.

Finding themselves trailing against the run of play, Liverpool simply lost their way for a short period of time and Cardiff's defence – expertly marshalled by Mark Hudson – comfortably kept Steven Gerrard and Co. at bay. With frustration creeping in and the Liverpool supporters looking somewhat worried, manager Dalglish introduced future Cardiff player Craig Bellamy into the action just before the hour mark and straightaway the whole complex of the game changed. Liverpool pressed more players forward and grabbed an equaliser on 60 minutes, although the Welsh 'super sub' had nothing to do with it.

Downing delivered a well-struck corner towards Carroll, whose header was flicked onto a post by Luis Suarez. Before any Cardiff defender could react, Liverpool's centre-back Skrtel got hold of the rebound to drive the ball between Heaton's legs. Liverpool were now in the driving seat but Cardiff held firm, refusing to crumble and, in fact, they created the better chances as the final headed towards extra time.

As expected, Cardiff's exertions began to catch up with them and when defender Mark Hudson was forced off with cramp Liverpool created a flurry of chances. Heaton tipped a Suarez shot just wide, Andrew Taylor clear a header from the Uruguayan off the line from the resulting corner, while Carroll, Bellamy and Johnson all narrowly missed the frame of the goal with good efforts.

In the 108th minute, Cardiff's defence finally cracked. Dirk Kuyt had a right-foot shot blocked by Anthony Gerrard (Hudson's replacement), but the ball came back to the Dutchman, who powered it with accuracy past Heaton. Liverpool 2 Cardiff City 1.

That was not the end of the action ... far from it. Kuyt was in the right position at the right time to kick away a goal-bound effort from Miller, as Cardiff threw caution to the wind. From the resulting corner, Liverpool 'keeper Reina, under some pressure with bodies all round him, simply couldn't stop Turner from bundling the ball over the line to take the final to penalties.

This is how the tense and nervous penalty shoot-out evolved, with Cardiff's Anthony Gerrard having the ill-luck to miss the vital tenth kick.

Gerrard (Liverpool) – missed 0-0
Miller (Cardiff) – missed 0-0
Adam (Liverpool) – missed 0-0
Cowie (Cardiff) – scored 0-1
Kuyt (Liverpool) – scored 1-1
Gestede (Cardiff) – missed 1-1
Downing (Liverpool) – scored 2-1
Whittingham (Cardiff) – scored 2-2
Johnson (Liverpool) – scored 3-2
Gerrard (Cardiff) – missed 3-2

It had been an extraordinary final, Stevie G saying, 'It was a really tough match. We were made to fight every inch of the way and all credit to Cardiff for a courageous effort. I also feel for my cousin, Anthony. It was a horrible moment for him to miss from the spot at such a crucial stage.'

NB: In terms of possession, City had 43 per cent to Liverpool 53 per cent. Seven of City's eleven goal attempts were on target against nineteen of Liverpool's thirty-nine. The Reds also had more corners than Cardiff – nineteen to three.

40

PREMIER LEAGUE
LIVERPOOL 3 EVERTON 0
13 March 2012

Steven Gerrard was declared fit to make his 400th senior appearance for Liverpool who, going into this, the 217th Merseyside derby, were in poor Premiership form, sitting in seventh position having lost five of their previous eight games, including three in a row, two coming against Arsenal and Manchester United.

Meanwhile, Everton, down in ninth position in the Premiership, were on a high after beating both the reigning champions Chelsea and Tottenham Hotspur in the recent weeks. Glen Johnson, who missed the previous League defeat by Sunderland, was still absent with a hamstring problem, allowing Martin Kelly to retain the right-back berth. Everton fan Jamie Carragher replaced Sebastian Coates at centre-back, while midfielder Charlie Adam was left out, allowing Jay Spearing to continue in centre of the park.

Reds manager Kenny Dalglish, still beaming over seeing his team lift the League Cup, said at a pre-match press conference: 'This Merseyside derby is always a cup final to Liverpool and Everton, and want to win it. My players will be ready to do battle and hopefully we can win again, to complete the double, having beaten our rivals 2-0 at Goodison Park earlier in the season.'

Liverpool (4-4-2): Reina, Kelly, Carragher, Skrtel, Enrique, Henderson (Kuyt), Gerrard, Spearing, Downing, Suarez, Carroll.
Everton (4-4-2): Howard, Hibbert, Distin, Jagielka, Baines, Coleman (Jelavic), Rodwell, Fellaini, Pienaar, Anichebe (Osman) Stracqualursi (Drenthe).
Attendance: 44,921

Everton boss David Moyes, celebrating his ten-year anniversary in charge, sprang a huge surprise by making six changes to the side that had beaten Spurs on Saturday. Evertonians still, to this day, wonder why so many alterations were made, particularly when many of those who came in failed to match the men they replaced. It was a poor decision. But did Liverpool care? No way. They went out to dominate the game from start to finish. From the moment Stevie G forced an acrobatic save from USA goalkeeper Tim Howard, and Jack Rodwell blocked

Jordan Henderson's follow up, Everton were always seemingly on the back foot. That set what was to be a predictably frantic tone, as tackles were traded from all quarters and the volume inside Anfield increased tenfold.

Earlier in the season Liverpool had failed several times when dominant, but on this occasion they were in no mood to let their opponents off the hook, producing their best home display since beating Newcastle United in late December. Gerrard fired his team in front, and rightly so, in the 34th minute. Some brilliant play by Luis Suarez set Martin Kelly free down the right and when the young right-back powerfully struck a shot that squirted away from Howard and Sylvain Distin failed to clear as Kelly followed up, Stevie G seized his moment, cleverly lofting a left-foot chip over a sea of blue shirts and into the unguarded net. The Anfield roar was deafening as a delighted Dalglish spun on his heels and thrust his arms to the sky. It was no more than Liverpool deserved and it was the response to the meek offering that they had produced against Sunderland 72 hours earlier.

Liverpool remained on top for the rest of the half and although Everton emerged after the interval looking more purposeful, the task soon went beyond them when superhero Gerrard thumped home his side's second goal to effectively end the contest. Suarez was the creator-in-chief with a wriggling, jinking run that carried him past three challenges before he teed up Gerrard to do the rest. His 10-yard blast sped past the grounded Howard like a guided missile and killed Everton stone dead.

With their advantage doubled, Liverpool were on fire and Andy Carroll should have extended the lead, but his left-foot drive whizzed past the outside of Howard's post. Kelly then came close, just failing to get on the end of another Downing centre, while Gerrard had another effort saved by the over-worked goalkeeper. The mood inside Anfield had changed dramatically since the last game there and Gerrard's smiles confirmed it as Everton boss Moyes had to endure chants of 'ten more years' from the home fans, who revelled in normal service being resumed.

The icing on the cake was duly applied in injury time. More clever play by the elusive Suarez, who was back to his best after serving a nine-match ban, caused havoc in the Everton defence. When he squared the ball to Gerrard, the midfielder gleefully smashed it home before giving the Kop an exultant three-finger salute.

Everton chief Moyes sat on the bench with his hands clasped together, shaking his head in disbelief. This was not the anniversary he planned. Not by a long shot. Liverpool had won in style, 'Star of the Show' Stevie G collected the match ball and Everton slipped out of Anfield a well beaten side.

41

FA CUP FINAL
CHELSEA 2 LIVERPOOL 1
5 May 2012

For Liverpool this was their fourteenth appearance in the FA Cup final; for Chelsea it was their eleventh. On paper the two teams were evenly matched, with the Reds lying eighth in the Premiership, two places below their London rivals.

En route to Wembley, Liverpool had ousted Oldham Athletic (5-1), Manchester United (2-1), Brighton and Hove Albion (6-1) and Stoke City (2-1) all at Anfield, along with Merseyside neighbours Everton 2-1 in the semi-final. Chelsea had knocked out Portsmouth, QPR, Birmingham City, Leicester City and Tottenham Hotspur in that order, scoring nineteen goals in six matches.

Steven Gerrard, who had missed three of the previous four Premiership games, was declared fit to play, along with defender Daniel Agger and front men Luis Suarez and Craig Bellamy. Chelsea brought back Ashley Cole and Juan Mata but there was no room for centre-backs David Luiz and Gary Cahill, or striker Fernando Torres. Interestingly, both Liverpool (0-1 to Fulham) and Chelsea (0-2 v. Newcastle) had lost their home Premiership games earlier in the week.

Chelsea (4-4-2): Čech, Bosingwa, Ivanovic, Terry, A. Cole, Ramires (Meireles), Lampard, Mikel, Mata (Malouda), Drogba, Kalou.
Liverpool (4-4-1-1): Reina, Johnson, Agger, Skrtel, Enrique, Gerrard, Henderson, Spearing (Carroll), Downing, Bellamy (Kuyt), Suarez.
Attendance: 89,102

The game itself was not great, but it was interesting as Chelsea survived a Liverpool fight-back to lift the coveted trophy for the third time in quick succession. Substitute Andy Carroll's brilliant second-half goal ensured it would be a close finish and although Liverpool pushed hard towards the end, Chelsea's defence held firm – just!

After a cagey opening 10 minutes, when eight midfield players were watchful of each other, the game burst into life with a goal out of nothing. Liverpool's young midfielder Jay Spearing lost possession to Mata near the halfway line and he paid a heavy price for his carelessness. The Spaniard raced clear and slipped in Brazilian Ramires, who held off José Enrique with surprising ease, before beating Pepe Reina at his near post with a confident, low shot. The goalkeeper admitted afterwards that he should have done better as the ball deflected into the net off his outstretched leg.

Liverpool were stunned and Gerrard was lucky not get yellow-carded after a scything tackle on Mata. Then Suárez attempted a speculative shot from the halfway line, but missed the target so badly that the ball went out for a throw in as hoots of derision echoed around the stadium.

At this point, Liverpool were playing with caution. Suárez was isolated up front while Craig Bellamy was not quite functioning as the main link between midfield and attack. Chelsea in fact, looked far more confident, especially in possession.

On the rare occasions when Liverpool got near to the Chelsea penalty area, Suárez and Stewart Downing were both guilty of giving the ball away in good positions, and despite a couple of typically determined runs from Gerrard, he was not quite delivering on all four cylinders.

For all their possession and after taking the lead, a hopeful 30-yard effort from Didier Drogba was all Chelsea could muster in the first half. Suárez also failed to take advantage of a sharp chance that fell to him, following a header by Jordan Henderson.

Liverpool started the second period far better than Chelsea and Gerrard's surging run came to a halt as he crashed to the ground in a vain attempt to win a penalty. Chelsea responded immediately and, after a lightning attack, Drogba claimed his eighth goal at Wembley to maintain his record of scoring in major competitive match. The move was simple and it took Liverpool totally by surprise!

Frank Lampard, given time and space, threaded a fine diagonal pass through to Drogba who took the ball in his stride, and before Martin Skrtel could close him down he beat Reina to his left with a low right-footer. It must be said that with his back to the Chelsea player, Skrtel didn't do a particularly good job in stopping Drogba from getting in a shot.

Liverpool reacted and Suárez brought a smart save from Petr Čech before manager Kenny Dalglish sent on Carroll for the tiring Spearing after 55 minutes, in an effort to boost their attacking options. Liverpool were now chasing the game as Gerrard sent a shot wide, while Salomon Kalou should have done better at the other end of the field, but missed the target by a mile with players in support on either side of him. Drogba was all set to try an extravagant strike from 30 yards but was stopped in his tracks when Suárez put his foot in the way and brought him down. Lampard fired the free-kick wide, and soon afterwards Drogba came close to increasing Chelsea's lead in their next attack.

Liverpool were under pressure but they somehow grabbed a lifeline with a fine goal from the hot £35-million striker Andy Carroll, and this one was much better than the one he scored in the semi-final against Everton. Controlling the ball in a yard or so inside the penalty area, he sent John Terry first one way then the other, before firing a left-foot rocket high past the startled Čech from the narrowest of angles.

With 25 minutes or so remaining, Liverpool were back in the match and they enjoyed their best spell during the next quarter of an hour, playing with self-belief and determination. Bellamy was getting more involved and Gerrard was revving himself up for one final surge. Indeed, the powerhouse in midfield raced onto a Carroll knockdown and attempted what would have been the most spectacular of equalisers, only to see his shot end up in the second tier of seats behind the goal.

Then, with the watch ticking down, Suarez fired the ball in and Carroll thought he had had squared things up with a powerful header from the Uruguayan's cross. Čech appeared to claw the ball back from behind the line and, despite the Liverpool bench celebrating, referee Phil Dowd allowed play to continue ... correctly as it turned out, since the immediate available replays did not establish that the ball had crossed the line.

Late on, with Chelsea on the back foot, John Terry blocked a terrific drive from Carroll who was gobsmacked not see the ball nestling in the back of the net, which would have taken the game into extra-time. To his credit, Liverpool boss Dalglish did not harp on about the incident afterwards, saying, 'If the officials got it right they deserve credit. We were excellent in the final half-hour but the game lasts for 90 minutes. You can't give a team as good as Chelsea a two-goal start.'

Roberto Di Matteo – the fourth Chelsea manager to win the FA Cup in six years – accepted it had been a tense finish. 'We played well for the majority of the game and scored two very nice goals, but it got a bit nervy towards the end,' he said. 'When Carroll came on he caused us some problems.' A disappointed Stevie G shrugged his shoulders and admitted, 'We didn't play well enough for the first hour and it cost us.' And commenting on Terry's last-ditch block, the Liverpool midfielder said, 'That's why he's in the team; he's a great defender!'

NB: Amazingly, three days after this final, Liverpool beat Chelsea 4-1 in a Premiership game at Anfield. Football's a funny old game!

42

EUROPEAN CHAMPIONSHIP, GROUP D
ENGLAND 3 SWEDEN 2
15 June 2012

England, having drawn 1-1 with France in their first Group D game, knew they had to beat Sweden in their second to stand any chance of qualifying for the quarter finals of the 2012 European championships. There were around 15,000 England fans inside Kiev's Olympic Stadium to see the game, as manager Roy Hodgson (without Wayne Rooney) still selected what he thought was an attacking line-up, with more options on the bench. The Swedes, who had lost their opening game 2-1 against Ukraine, could afford to lose.

England (4-4-2): Hart, G. Johnson, Terry, Lescott, A. Cole, Milner (Walcott), Gerrard, Parker, A. Young, Carroll, Welbeck (Oxlade-Chamberlain).
Sweden (4-4-2): Isaksson, Granqvist (Lustig), Mellberg, J. Olsson, M. Olsson, Larsson, Svensson, Källström, Elm (Wilhelmsson), Ibrahimovic, Elmander (Rosenberg).
Attendance: 64,640

Hodgson started with Andy Carroll alongside Danny Welbeck while Ashley Young began proceedings on the left flank. In contrast, Sweden's boss Enrik Hamren asked Johan Elmander to be Zlatan Ibrahimović's foil up front. England began brightly and Scott Parker's early drive forced Swedish 'keeper Andreas Isaksson into a smart save. However, Sweden looked good in possession and Sebastian Larsson tested his one-time Birmingham City clubmate Joe Hart with a well-struck drive. Glen Johnson then did exceptionally well to thwart the pony-tailed Ibrahimović, who looked set to score when clean through on goal, and soon afterwards Hart was well positioned to deny the Sweden captain.

It was the England captain, though, who created the opening goal on 23 minutes. Steven Gerrard pinged a long, diagonal cross from the right side of midfield straight to the unmarked Carroll who cleverly headed home from the centre of the penalty area. It took Sweden quite a while to regroup, but when they did, the dangerous Ibrahimović embarked on a solo run, only for Hart to stop his deflected shot. Meanwhile, at the other end of the field, Ashley Young dragged an effort into the side netting.

Sweden were now being restricted to long range shots and Kim Källström came close as they ended the first half strongly, although just before the interval Danny Welbeck was stopped in his tracks by a superb tackle from Olaf Mellberg.

It was Mellberg who was responsible for Sweden's equaliser 4 minutes into the second half. Ibrahimović saw his free-kick blocked but he leapt up to volley the ball to the former Aston Villa defender, whose close range effort hit Johnson via Hart's gloves, and rolled into the net despite the right-back's desperate lunge to keep the ball out.

With 18,000 fans behind them – unusually outnumbering England supporters – Sweden sensed victory by going for England's jugular, and it was that man Mellberg who was at the heart of things again, rising high to head Larsson's free-kick firmly past Hart. With England on the back burner, Ibrahimović, sprinting clear, so nearly scored a third, but the alert Hart was in the right position to save his weak effort.

England somehow withstood the pressure and in the 63rd minute almost grabbed an equaliser, Isaksson pulling off a smart reflex save from John Terry's header. However, from the resulting corner, the unsighted 'keeper was beaten by a long-distance right-footed effort from Theo Walcott, who had only been on the field for a matter of minutes.

Both teams were now going flat out for victory; the unmarked Källström fired fractionally over and Hart denied Ibrahimović with a stunning save. It was end to end stuff; anyone could win, and with less than a quarter of an hour remaining, England got their third and final goal.

Welbeck, losing his marker, moved swiftly into position with his back to goal, before cleverly flicking the ball home from 6 yards. As he celebrated, his face was a picture of sheer joy; this was his first competitive goal in his seventh game for England.

Late on, Stevie G was denied by Isaksson from point-blank range, but it mattered not. England had won – just. Gerrard said, 'Sweden were better than France and we had to work hard for our victory.'

NB: By losing, Sweden went out of the competition. England went on to beat Ukraine 1-0 in their final group game but then crashed out to Italy on penalties in the quarter-finals.

43

2014 WORLD CUP QUALIFIER
ENGLAND 1 UKRAINE 1
11 September 2012

Ukraine, managed by the former Russian international Oleg Blokhin, looked good at times when they had lost 1-0 to England in Donetsk, in Euro 2012, a few months earlier. Indeed, England chief Roy Hodgson said at the time, 'They will be formidable opponents in this Group. I know we will be without John Terry, Wayne Rooney and Theo Walcott, but I can still field a strong team.'

Prior to this qualifying encounter, the two countries had met each other on five occasions, with England winning four and Ukraine one. And of course England were in decent form, having comfortably defeated Moldova 5-0 in a qualifying game in Chisinau just four days earlier.

England (4-4-1-1): Hart, Johnson, Lescott, Jagielka, Baines (Bertrand), Milner, Gerrard, Lampard, Cleverley (Welbeck), Oxlade-Chamberlain (Sturridge), Defoe.
Ukraine (4-3-2-1): Pyatov, Selin (Shevchuk), Khacheridi, Rakitskiy, Tymoschuk, Garmash, Zozulya (Devic), Gusev, Konoplienka, Yarmolenko, Rotan (Nazarenko).
Attendance: 68,102

Ukraine's robust approach was emphasised in the opening moments when a bone-shaking collision between Steven Gerrard and Roman Zozulya left the England's captain limping heavily.

The visitors were in no mood to take a backward step and they almost went ahead when Oleg Gusev's deflected cross looped over goalkeeper Joe Hart, only to drift to safety off an upright.

England, who had been struggling to exert any sort of influence in midfield, thought they had broken through Ukraine's tight defence in the 11th minute when Jermain Defoe turned on the edge of the area before striking a 20-yarder past Andriy Pyatov. Unfortunately for the Tottenham striker, Turkish referee Cuneyt Cakir disallowed the goal, indicating that the Spurs striker had pushed Andriy Yarmolenko prior to shooting.

Ukraine continued to threaten and it required a goalline clearance from Gerrard after Ruslan Rotan's effort eluded Hart. Finding it hard to cope with the superior technique of Ukraine, England did manage a few openings as the half progressed – the best of which fell to Cleverley, who shot straight at Pyatov from barely 8 yards after Defoe had knocked Gerrard's cross into his path.

It proved an expensive miss as Ukraine took the lead 6 minutes before the interval. Joleon Lescott conceded possession rather cheaply, and when the ball found its way to Konoplianka he was able to bend a superb effort high past Hart from 25 yards, despite a desperate challenge from the aggressive Gerrard. There is no doubt that Ukraine deserved their lead. They dominated possession for long periods during the first half and could easily have scored a couple more goals.

England responded well and created two opportunities in a short space of time, both of which fell to Cleverley. Unfortunately he was unable to take either, mis-shooting badly from a good position in front of goal and then hitting the outside of the post when perhaps he should have done better. That second effort was to be his last significant contribution as he was replaced by his clubmate Danny Welbeck just after the hour mark. Then, just after Johnson had fired narrowly wide, Daniel Sturridge came on for out-of-sorts Alex Oxlade-Chamberlain. Almost immediately Welbeck came close to equalising when he struck the woodwork, leaving manager Hodgson holding his head in sheer frustration on the touchline.

The Manchester United front man had certainly given England a fillip and he became the central figure again as their pressure at last produced a goal, albeit from the penalty spot.

In the 87th minute, Yevgen Khacherdi handled as Welbeck threatened again, leaving Frank Lampard to confidently score his 26th international goal from 12 yards to equal Bryan Robson's record for a midfielder.

There was still time for a setback for England, however, when hard-working skipper Steven Gerrard, who had earlier received a yellow card for catching Rotan with his elbow, was sent off after a clumsy challenge on Denys Garmash. Thankfully, his dismissal came right at the end of the game and England's ten men had no worries about holding on for a draw that they just about deserved.

As a result of his red card, Gerrard missed the qualifier against San Marino the following month. After the game, former Liverpool defender Mark Lawrenson told Stevie G that a draw was a real bonus. 'When you don't play well and pinch a point, you begin to think it could just turn out to be a very good result. The way Ukraine celebrated at the end meant that this was a big result for them … and they could have had so much more.'

In contrast, there was relief on the face of England boss Roy Hodgson, who clearly accepted a point, saying, 'This is the best my injury and illness hit team was going to get from a tough night's work. It's a far cry from the easy 5-0 win we achieved against Moldova in Chisinau on Friday.'

44

PREMIER LEAGUE
NEWCASTLE UNITED 0 LIVERPOOL 6
27 April 2013

The spotlight prior to this game had been focused on Liverpool's Uruguayan striker Luis Suarez for biting Chelsea's Branislav Ivanovic at Anfield six days earlier. Even Prime Minister David Cameron intervened, saying that he had set 'The most appalling example' to children.

Liverpool's leading scorer at the time, with thirty goals to his name, was also on the shortlist for the PFA's Player of the Year award, but he would not play again for the Reds until September 2013 after being handed a ten-game ban. This led to a fierce response from Liverpool who said they are 'shocked and disappointed' at the punishment.

A three-man independent and neutral regulatory commission opted for the lengthy suspension after considering the Football Association's charge of violent conduct against a written submission from the Anfield club on Wednesday morning. An FA statement said, 'A three-person independent regulatory commission today upheld the FA's claim that a suspension of three matches was clearly insufficient and the player will serve a further seven first-team matches in addition to the standard three. The suspension begins with immediate effect.'

For the game at Newcastle (lying sixteenth in the table), Liverpool (seventh position) brought back Daniel Sturridge (he had been on the subs' bench against Chelsea) in an otherwise unchanged team. Defenders Martin Kelly, John Flanigan and midfielder Joe Allen were all out injured. Having lost only one of their previous nine Premiership games, Liverpool were confident of winning on Tyneside and Steven Gerrard said, 'We'll be up for this one after hearing of Luis's ban.'

Newcastle United (4-4-1-1): Elliot, Yanga-M'Biwa, Perch (Ben Arfa), Haidara, Debuchy, S. Taylor , Cabaye, Sissoko, Gutierrez (Gouffran), Tiote (Anita), Cisse.
Liverpool (4-3-2-1): Reina, Johnson, Carragher, Agger, Enrique, Gerrard (Borini), Henderson, Lucas, Downing Courtinho (Suso), Sturridge (Shelvey).
Attendance: 52,351

As it was, Liverpool barely missed Suarez in the game, completely outplaying a relegation-facing Newcastle. Defender Daniel Agger's looping header and Jordan

Henderson's first-half, smart finish set the Reds on the way to their biggest Premiership victory of the season.

During a rather one-sided second period, which saw United's French international defender Mathieu Debuchy sent off for going 'straight through' Philippe Coutinho with a two-footed lunge, striker Daniel Sturridge netted twice from close range, Fabio Borini slipped in his first League goal and Henderson bagged his second from the free-kick awarded for Debuchy's red-card offence.

This was Newcastle's heaviest top-flight home defeat since September 1925 when they crashed 7-1 to Blackburn, while for Liverpool it was their best league win on the road for a decade, since beating West Brom by the same score (6-0) in April 2003. Coutinho was pushed forward to assist Sturridge and he certainly added imagination and spark to Liverpool's attack. His excellent pass set to Glen Johnson sprinting down the right inside the opening minute almost produced a goal.

Two good chances fell to Sturridge soon afterwards, before Agger, all alone on the edge of the 6-yard box, directed Stewart Downing's flighted cross into the net in the 3rd minute. A rampant Liverpool then doubled their advantage on 17 minutes. The industrious Coutinho was the architect with a precise pass that cut through the home defence to find Sturridge. He unselfishly rolled the ball to Henderson, who gleefully side-footed it into the far corner of Rob Elliot's net. It was as simple as that.

Only a James Perch header troubled Liverpool during the first-half, which ended with a chorus of boos from the home supporters towards their dejected players as they trudged off the pitch.

Manager Alan Pardew introduced Hatem Ben Arfa and Yoan Gouffran for the start of the second half but the substitutes had little time to make an impact before Liverpool shot into a 3-0 lead on 54 minutes. Unable to cope with Coutinho's directness, Newcastle's defence was stretched to its limit as the Brazilian's exquisite pass sent Sturridge clear to score with consummate ease.

Then, a well-drilled move involving Gerrard and Henderson comfortably sprang the offside trap, allowing Sturridge a simple tap in for his second and Liverpool's fourth goal on the hour. It was one-way traffic that some Newcastle fans couldn't bear to watch, and hundreds began to make their way to the exit doors, muttering 'What a load of rubbish.' It soon got even worse for the Magpies supporters that remained inside the ground when Italian Fabio Borini, who had replaced Gerrard, got on the scoresheet with only his second touch of the ball. Downing eased past Papiss Cisse and found Borini hovering menacingly inside the box. The striker quickly adjusted his feet before driving a low shot beyond the diving Elliot.

Deflated and totally bemused, Newcastle were then forced to play the remaining 15 minutes with ten men when Debuchy received his second yellow card of the match for a two-footed challenge on the mightily impressive Coutinho.

Henderson dutifully placed the ball down for the free-kick before jogging up to curl a beauty past Elliot. Borini and Coutinho had chances to increase Liverpool's lead late on before referee Andre Marriner blew the final whistle to end Newcastle day of shear misery!

45

PREMIER LEAGUE
MANCHESTER UNITED 0 LIVERPOOL 3
16 March 2014

Second-place Liverpool, unbeaten in nine Premiership games and only two defeats in fifteen games, went into this vital encounter at Old Trafford full of confidence. Having beaten their rivals at Anfield 1-0 earlier in the season, the double was there for the taking! United were lying sixth in the table. They were not playing at all well, having won only four of their previous nine Premiership games. They had also been dumped out of the FA Cup by Swansea City in the third round and by Sunderland in the semi-finals of the League Cup, but they were still in the Champions League – just!

Liverpool boss Brendan Rodgers had virtually a full squad to choose from. With thirty goals scored in their nine Premiership games since Boxing Day, the goals had been flying fin with Daniel Sturridge and Luis Suarez both on fire. Indeed, Reds' 'SAS' combination had scored forty-two times between them, and Steven Gerrard had contributed eight in the twenty-eight Premier League games played by Liverpool up to this game with United. As the supporters, and a few players said at the time: 'Bring 'em on.'

Manchester United (4-4-2): De Gea, Rafael, Jones, Vidic, Evra, Fellaini (Cleverley), Carrick, Mata (Ferdinand), Rooney, Januzaj (Welbeck), Van Persie.
Liverpool: Mignolet, Johnson, Skrtel, Agger, Flanagan, Henderson, Gerrard (Lucas), Allen, Sterling (Coutinho), Sturridge (Aspas), Suarez.
Attendance: 75,225

This resulted in a stupendous victory for Liverpool. Admittedly United were woeful and had defender Nemanja Vidic sent-off, but let's be honest, Steven Gerrard and Co. were very good, handing out a footballing lesson to David Moyes' men. Liverpool were much sharper, had a better-equipped defence, a more livelier and enterprising midfield and a brilliant strike-force. Only Wayne Rooney and goalkeeper David De Gea, who pulled off several fine saves, earned their wages for the bedraggled United team!

From start to finish, Liverpool looked the more purposeful side, with local-born left-back Jon Flanagan, in particular, looking a real star of the future. He had been sent off in a reserve match at Old Trafford twelve months earlier for a minor challenge on Adnan Januzaj and was first to go into the book in this game, but that didn't stop him from giving everything he had right through to the final whistle.

Steven Gerrard was also very much a man on a mission and he too worked his socks off, as did Suarez and Sturridge, Raheem Sterling, the gutsy Joe Allen and Jordan Henderson.

As it was, United were abysmal, being completely out-done by a Liverpool side that passed the ball with speed and intelligence, and if they had taken three or four of the chances that came their way the final scoreline might well have read 6-0, 7-0, or even 8-0.

Gerrard even missed the opportunity of bagging a hat-trick of penalties when he struck De Gea's right-hand post with his third spot kick, having already netted twice from 12 yards.

Tactically superior, Liverpool, with a midfield diamond, which allowed Sterling to operate behind Suarez and Sturridge, wreaked havoc in United's wobbly defence. If referee Mark Clattenburg had been strong enough, Liverpool could have been awarded five penalties, not three, as Phil Jones and Marouane Fellaini both nibbled at Suarez's ankles. Gerrard was superb in everything he did (and tried), being ably assisted in the engine room by Henderson and Allen.

After a solid half-hour in which they dominated possession, Liverpool deservedly went in front in the 34th minute when United's right-back Rafael da Silva handled inside the box as Suarez went round him. The Brazilian had already been yellow-carded but was let off by Clattenburg, when realistically he should have been walking down the tunnel. Gerrard made no mistake from the spot. For Liverpool, that decision did not matter a great deal as Juan Mata and Fellaini, Moyes' two big signings, were at this point being overrun in centre-field while Januzaj was having his worst game of the season. When Fellaini was substituted, rebellious cheers ran out from the crowd.

With Liverpool in total control, Gerrard blasted in his second penalty early in the second half after Phil Jones had bundled over Allen, who was running on to Henderson's pass. Just like his first, Stevie G – who was voted Man of the Match – took the second brilliantly, netting low down near to De Gea's left-hand post. On the third occasion, however, he chose to fire the ball the other way and misjudged his shot.

The third penalty came about when Sturridge appeared to dive over Vidic's sprawling challenge, but referee Clattenburg saw it differently and pointed to the spot before sending off the United centre-back. Liverpool boss Rodgers admitted after the game that it was 'harsh' on the defender, adding 'you win some, you lose some and over the course of the season usually things cancel each other out.'

Trailing by two, United were hopelessly lost in the final quarter of an hour. They couldn't string two passes together and Liverpool's dominance was confirmed 6 minutes from time when Suárez controlled Sturridge's miscued shot to complete United's misery. Sturridge had a chance late but by this time United had given up and the ground was half empty.

There had been a 43-point swing in Liverpool's favour between the two teams over a twelve month period and, on the evidence of this victory, Liverpool were high in confidence, the momentum was with them and as the players left the Old Trafford pitch, they could hear their fans chanting: 'We're going to win the League.' Unfortunately it was not to be!

46

PREMIER LEAGUE
LIVERPOOL 0 CHELSEA 2
27 April 2014

For a number of reasons, this was a huge game of football. Pundits said that if Liverpool (on an eleven-match League-winning run at the time) won, they would become Premiership champions; if Chelsea should claim victory they would be back in the title race, while a draw would suit the Merseysiders and certainly give the other title chasers, Manchester City, a massive boost.

Former Chelsea striker Daniel Sturridge was missing from Liverpool's attack but another ex-Blues star, right-back Glen Johnson, was in. And Steven Gerrard was all set to fight it out in midfield with his England colleague Frank Lampard, as well as do battle with fellow internationals Ashley Cole and perhaps ex-Anfield favourite Fernando Torres.

Liverpool (4-4-2): Mignolet, Johnson, Skrtel, Sakho, Flanagan (Laso Aspas), Lucas (Sturridge), Gerrard, Allen, Courtinho, Sterling, Suarez.
Chelsea (4-5-1): Schwarzer, Azpilicueta, Ivanovic, Kalas, A. Cole, Lampard, Matic, Mikel, Salah (Willian), Demba Ba (Torres), Schurrle (Cahill).
Attendance: 44,726

In their previous five home games, Liverpool had scored their first goal in the 1st, 3rd, 39th, 2nd and 6th minutes respectively. It was clear what Chelsea needed to do – keep a clean sheet in the first half and victory could be theirs! As it transpired, Chelsea manager José Mourinho got his tactics spot on to keep alive his side's hopes of an unlikely double and put a damper on Liverpool's challenge. With Gerrard and his teammates committed to attack, the visitors relied on defending and it was the latter that succeeded!

By time-wasting and breaking up play, Chelsea denied Liverpool any sort of opportunity to get into their rhythm. It was a classic Mourinho destruction and frustration ploy, which infuriated Liverpool so much so that at one point Gerrard was engaged in a bit of push and shove with the Chelsea boss in trying to get the ball back into play while Luis Suarez stood to applaud goalkeeper Mark Schwarzer for time-wasting. Referee Martin Atkinson certainly made it clear he was aware of the tactic by pointing to his watch to intimate that he was adding on time, but he did not take decisive action in actually booking anyone until stoppage time.

Ashley Cole had an early shot parried by Simon Mignolet but Chelsea were happy to concede possession and territory as Liverpool pushed menacingly forward whenever possible.

Full-back Johnson's crisp shot was deflected behind; Philippe Courtinho volleyed Suarez's cross into the side-netting; the well-positioned and alert Cole cleared off the line; and when the ball bounced down off John Obi Mikel, the unmarked Mamadou Sakho blazed his effort over the top.

Shouts for handball against Jon Flanagan were waved aside, while at the other end Suarez failed to capitalise on a rare mistake by Cole by curling his right-footed shot over. However, on the stroke of half-time, with Chelsea under pressure, Demba Ba was not as wasteful! A harmless looking ball was collected by Gerrard, who suddenly slipped when in possession, allowing the Chelsea striker to run on and score low past Mignolet in fine style.

After the break, Schwarzer produced a terrific diving save to keep out a first-time effort from Joe Allen, which was followed by an even better stop by Mignolet who denied André Schurrle.

Gerrard tried his utmost to make up for his mistake and redress the balance, but twice in quick succession the England man found Schwarzer with direct and well-struck shots from outside the area and once with a deliberate header from inside it.

Substitute Sturridge, returning to action after a hamstring injury, never really looked like breaking through Chelsea's thick blue line and, after Suarez's late volley was punched over by Schwarzer, the game ended with a jubilant Mourinho charging down the touchline to celebrate substitute Willian's breakaway goal which gave his side a 2-0 victory.

Liverpool, with 73 per cent of the play, had twenty-six attempts at goal to Chelsea's eleven eight of which were on target against four by the visitors. The Reds also gained fourteen corners to Chelsea's two. But as they say, goals win matches – I have to say it, this victory was all down to the brilliant tactics employed by Jose Mourinho.

As it was, Liverpool could still win the title. They had two games left, away to Crystal Palace and at home Newcastle United, and they had to win them both!

47

PREMIER LEAGUE

CRYSTAL PALACE 3 LIVERPOOL 3
5 May 2014

Liverpool knew they had to win this, their penultimate game of the Premiership season. It was as simple as that. Let's be truthful about it, a draw or a defeat would surely, to all intents and purposes, end their title hopes for good!

Crystal Palace (4-4-2): Speroni, Mariappa, Ward, Dikgacoi (Ince), Dann, Delaney, Puncheon (Gayle), Ledley, Jedinak, Chamakh (Murray), Bolasie.
Liverpool (4-4-2): Mignolet, Johnson, Flanagan, Skrtel, Sakho, Gerrard, Lucas, Allen, Sterling, (Coutinho), Sturridge (Moses), Suarez.
Attendance: 25,261

With referee Mark Clattenburg in charge, Liverpool started strongly against Tony Pulis's rather uncommitted Crystal Palace side suspiciously in end-of-season mode. The Eagles looked vulnerable and slightly dishevelled as Steven Gerrard, Joe Allen and the Brazilian Lucas began to marshall the midfield zone with authority.

Three chances were created before Allen – hardly a player known for his aerial prowess – made the vital breakthrough in the 18th minute by heading home direct from Gerrard's well-struck corner. With Palace on the back foot, Liverpool poured forward and on three occasions before half-time, chances went begging as at three unsteady looking home defenders simply lost their bearings!

With Liverpool totally in control, it came as no real surprise when Daniel Sturridge made it 2-0 in the 53rd minute. He controlled Gerrard's long pass perfectly, turned inside Joel Ward and shot hard and straight at goal, the ball taking a slight, yet decisive deflection off Damien Delaney before ending up in the net. Some reports have listed this as an own goal. 90 seconds later it was 3-0 when Luis Suárez played a smart one-two with Raheem Sterling before going on to beat Argentine goalkeeper Julian Speroni comfortably. At this point thousands of travelling Liverpool's fans started blazing out their victory songs. But things were to change dramatically in that last quarter of an hour. In fact, it all happened in the space of barely 10 minutes – 596 seconds to be precise!

Completely out of the blue, Delaney smashed in a terrific 20-yard shot that deflected off Glen Johnson to find the top corner of Mignolet's net in the 79th minute. Then, 100 seconds or so a later, in their next worthwhile attack and with the Selhurst Park faithful roaring them on, the Eagles 'soared' again to stun Liverpool for a second time. Yannick Bolasie's brilliant run on the left set up substitute Dwight Gayle, who belted the ball past the stranded Mignolet. It was now 2-3 – game on. With Liverpool looking shell-shocked, Palace drove forward and it was Gayle again in the 88th minute who completed an amazing comeback by scoring his second goal of the night. With an instant pass, Glenn Murray split open the Liverpool defence again, allowing Gayle to go on and beat Mignolet with consummate ease.

Three goals up and now level, Liverpool desperately tried to add another twist to this extraordinary game, but one felt that the damage had been done. For a few seconds after the third Palace goal had gone in, Liverpool boss Brendan Rodgers closed his eyes. 'We got carried away,' he said afterwards. 'We thought we could score more and we lost our defensive structure.' Even at 3-3, rampant Palace, throwing caution to the wind, had two more chances to score and if they had it would have been one of the most remarkable comeback victories in Premiership history.

Reporter Daniel Harvey wrote in *The Guardian*,

It was naivety, to put it another way! Rodgers accepted that the title was surely heading to Manchester but the players had already done that without even speaking. Martin Skrtel was on the floor, pulling his fingers down his face. Stevie G went to comfort Suárez. In the end Kolo Touré, an unused substitute, led the striker off the pitch. To a man, it was a picture of sporting desolation.

It had been a quite incredible finale but all credit to Palace for a stunning effort. They had been completely outplayed for an hour at least but kept on trying. They hardly got a look in during a rather one-sided first half, as Liverpool's goalkeeper Simon Mignolet had precious little to do other than collect a couple of long-range efforts from Jason Puncheon and Mile Jedinak.

In fact, Mignolet's goal wasn't unduly threatened until those late, dramatic moments when everything unravelled and Palace's resurgence and resilience earned them a point. All credit to Gayle, Palace had a couple of half-chances to win the match. As it was, it seemed almost irrelevant that Liverpool had gone back to the top of the league.

At the final whistle Steven Gerrard dropped on his haunches. All around him there were Liverpool players in a state of shock; some fell to the turf, others just starred at each other aimlessly. Luis Suárez pulled his shirt over his face as he tried to hide the tears, while Stevie G pushed away the television cameras as he battled to keep in his own emotions under control. They were a broken lot.

Manchester City leapfrogged over Liverpool after beating Aston Villa and with another home game to come after that, against West Ham United at the Etihad Stadium, Manuel Pellegrini's side were now clear favourites to win the Premier League title. It would need something extraordinary to happen to prevent City from becoming champions for the second time in three seasons. For Liverpool the tears were flowing in the stands and on the pitch. They knew it was over.

48

WORLD CUP, GROUP D
COSTA RICA 0 ENGLAND 0
24 June 2014

Having lost 2-1 to both Italy and Uruguay in their first two group games, England desperately wanted to give their travelling supporters something to cheer about when they met unbeaten Costa Rica in Belo Horizonte – the venue where, sixty-four years earlier, Walter Winterbottom's England side had been humiliated 1-0 by the USA.

Manager Roy Hodgson, disappointed with the team's performances so far, rang the changes, retaining only two players – Cahill and Sturridge – from the previous game, naming Steven Gerrard on the bench (in what was to be his last appearance in an England shirt), along with his Anfield colleague Raheem Sterling and Wayne Rooney. This was to be the first-ever meeting against Costa Rica and England wanted to make it a winning one.

Costa Rica (4-4-2): Navas, Gamboa, Duarte, Gonzales, Miller, Diaz, Ruiz, Borges (Barrantes), Tejeda, Brenes (Bolanos), Campbell (Uranda).
England (4-3-2-1): Foster, Jones, Smalling, Cahill, Shaw, Lampard, Wilshere (Gerrard), Milner (Rooney), Barkley, Lallana (Sterling), Sturridge.
Attendance: 57,823

Let's put things into perspective: this was not a very good game of football, as summed up neatly by the BBC's Chief football writer Phil McNulty, who wrote,

England's World Cup ended without even the scant consolation of a victory as they played out a tame draw with Costa Rica. This was a dead rubber ... and there was nothing on show here to offer any belated cheer at the end of a miserable tournament. Costa Rica's status as the surprise package of Group D was cemented by a result that ensured they finished top – and will face Greece in Recife on Sunday.

Apart from the first quarter of an hour, which they totally dominated, England never really looked like winning. They had a few openings now and again, and if they had managed to take perhaps one of them, they might, just might, have won. Daniel Sturridge missed a couple at least and Lampard and Lallana also had sniffs at goal, prompting Hodgson to say after the game:

> We created chances and that's important. I'm not concerned about Sturridge!; he'll take goal chances in the future. I thought we were really unlucky not to win this game. I thought the whole back four was absolutely excellent. We restricted Costa Rica to almost no chances. In midfield we dominated and outplayed them.

Well, the truth is that England didn't lose – thanks possibly to goalkeeper Ben Foster who brilliantly tipped Celso Borges' free-kick on to the bar in the first half. This was all he had to do in the entire 90 minutes! I'm sorry to say, but this was a game England should have won, and they should never have lost to Italy or Uruguay either.

Hodgson gave Frank Lampard the captain's armband and it was the Chelsea man who made the first telling tackle. England were lucky not to concede early on when Joel Campbell's shot was certainly deflected narrowly wide by Gary Cahill, although the referee awarded a goal kick.

Sturridge then fired just wide from 20 yards after good control, before the same player headed over from 6 yards after Phil Jones had knocked Ross Barkley's corner back into the danger zone.

Sturridge also had a good claim for a penalty ignored when he went down under the challenge of Oscar Duarte, but referee Djamal Haimoudi waved play on.

The lively Sturridge had England's first opportunity of the second half but the Liverpool striker's control let him down and 'keeper Keylor Navas was able to block his effort, sustaining a nasty knock in the process. All of England's best chances were falling to Sturridge and he was off target yet again, curling Jack Wilshere's flick wide of the far post. Hodgson then made three substitutions in quick succession, sending on Raheem Sterling, Gerrard and Rooney, the latter announcing his arrival with a clever chip that required a fine save from Navas.

But there were to be no goals, no more chances in fact, and certainly no glory for England. This was a poor game. I'll say no more.

One poster held up by an England fan, read 'Always look on the bright side of life.' ... Quite right, mate.

NB: This was England's 11th goalless draw in World Cup football – the most by any nation. This fiftieth and final defining game was included simply because it brought to an end Steven Gerrard's fourteen-year career as an England player. Since his debut in May 2000, he had appeared in 114 full international (one fewer than David Beckham), making him his country's second most capped outfield player at that time. Goalkeeper Peter Shilton, with 125 caps, holds the overall record.

49

CHAMPIONS LEAGUE (GROUP)
LIVERPOOL 1 FC BASEL 1
9 December 2014

The atmosphere, the build-up, the tension leading up to this final group game of the 2014/15 Champions League competition was something special. Steven Gerrard said, 'We're hungry for success ... and if we can get into the knockout stages we can shock the best in Europe. This will be a nerve-racking encounter, I'm sure of that, but with the backing of our fans I'm sure we can make it through.'

There had been times during the previous decade when an evening game at Anfield was something special – this one against the Swiss champions was another! Brendan Rodgers' side had taken just four points from five games in their group, which had been dominated by Real Madrid (fifteen from a possible fifteen), but he knew, as did the players, that victory in front of their home fans would see them into the knockout stages.

Rodgers was quick to state: 'We must win – that's all that matters tonight'. Skipper Steven Gerrard, ten years to the month after scoring that 'extra special' goal against Olympiakos (also in a final group game), declared himself fit to return to the side that had played out a dire 0-0 draw with Sunderland at the weekend. He would be asked to play a more forward role to assist Rickie Lambert.

It was announced shortly before kick-off that Basel's experienced Argentine centre-back Walter Samuel would be on the bench, along with Chile's World Cup midfielder Marcelo Diaz and young striker Breel Embolo. However, veteran hitman (and skipper) Marco Streller would lead the line, with Fabian Schar lining up in defence.

It was common knowledge that the Reds had struggled at Anfield all season and even the most diehard supporters were hoping and praying that things would be 'alright on the night' this time round, but some were optimistic, to say the least. Even ex-player Jamie Carragher said: 'It will be tough.'

Liverpool (4-4-1-1): Mignolet, Johnson, Skrtel, Lovren, Enrique (Moreno), Lucas (Courtinho), Allen, Henderson, Gerrard, Sterling, Lambert (Markovic).
FC Basel (4-5-1): Vaclik Xhaka, Schar, Suchy, Safari, Eleney (Diaz), Frei, Zuffi Samuel), Gonzales, Gashi, Streller (Embola).
Attendance: 43,290

As it happened, it wasn't a happy night on Merseyside as Liverpool's wretched Champions League campaign came to a disappointing conclusion. They failed to beat Basel and as a result their hopes of reaching the knockout phase evaporated.

Skipper Steven Gerrard – who had dragged Liverpool through to victory in a similar situation a decade ago – threatened to do so again when his brilliant late free-kick equalised Fabian Frei's first-half goal for the Swiss. But it was not to be. In fact, until Gerrard's terrific equaliser, the usually noisy Kop had been silent for long periods, except when voicing frustration at Rodgers' side that had lost its way since coming so close to winning the Premier League in 2013/14. Liverpool may claim some injustice following the dismissal of substitute Lazar Markovic who was delivering a promising cameo, but Fabian Frei's first-half goal and the subsequent 1-1 draw put them out and into the Europa League instead.

Around 3,000 Basel's fans were in noisy and buoyant mood despite a Merseyside downpour before kick-off, and they certainly had plenty to applaud and admire as their team played with a lot of assurance and skill during the first 45 minutes. When the half-time whistle came, the ardent Anfield audience simply looked on in total frustration and silence. BBC's chief sports reporter Phil McNulty wrote: 'Instead of coming out with pace, energy, movement and the sort of threat befitting the task in front of them, Liverpool were nervous and slower than Basel, who took a deserved lead after 25 minutes.'

After a slick exchange of passes with Luca Zuffi, Frei's low but precise shot from the edge of the penalty area beat the motionless Simon Mignolet. At this point Liverpool's defence looked hesitant and the goal they conceded, instead of sparking the midfield and front men into action, only added to Basel's confidence, for a good ten minutes looking the more likely side to score again.

Liverpool simply couldn't muster a worthwhile attack and even a frustrated Gerrard gesticulated with two of his teammates after another breakdown in communication. As a result, Rodgers was forced into a double substitution at the start of the second half. Left-back Jose Enrique and striker Rickie Lambert were replaced by Alberto Moreno and Markovic. The latter finally injected some life into Liverpool's game before his stupid sending off just after the hour mark.

Liverpool simply couldn't carve a way through the well-organised Basel back four, although Dutch referee Bjorn Kuipers infuriated the Kop in ignoring loud appeals for a penalty when Gerrard was sent tumbling, as he went for a loose ball with visiting goalkeeper Tomas Vaclik.

Just as hope seemed to be slipping away, it was superhero Gerrard who delivered once again. Liverpool won a free-kick 20 yards out and with superb technique Stevie G sent his free-kick into the top right hand corner of the flying Vaclik's net, just inside the post.

It was game on, at last and, as the pressure and the noise levels increased, the well-positioned Vaclik showed great athleticism to clutch Jordan Henderson's deflected header just as it seemed as the ball would bounce over the line in front of an expectant Kop. In a predictably frenzied finish, defender Martin Skrtel was pushed up front as a last throw of the dice. He was only fractionally off target with a near-post flick, while the impressive Vaclik once again denied Henderson with a fine diving save, as well as denying Raheem Sterling.

As the minutes, and then seconds, time Basel simply shut up shop and comfortably held on for a draw.

BBC's reporter Phil McNulty said:

> It was tough to compile a strong case for Liverpool deserving to get out of this group. This has been a wretched Champions League campaign, with only one win from six games. On that basis there can be no complaints from manager Brendan Rodgers or his players.

As it was, Liverpool duly entered the long running Europa League competition and were immediately paired with Turkish club Besiktas in the first knockout round.

50

LEAGUE CUP SEMI-FINAL, 2nd LEG
CHELSEA 1 LIVERPOOL 0
(lost 2-1 on aggregate)
27 January 2015

After being held 1-1 in the first leg at Anfield, Liverpool knew they would have to produce a top-class performance in the second leg at Stamford Bridge if they wanted to reach their 12th League Cup final. Manager Brendan Rodgers admitted to the press that he would field 'an attacking line-up', with Raheem Sterling as his main front man. Steven Gerrard, Coutinho and Markovic would get forward as often as possible and even Alberto Moreno would be asked to attack when possible down the left.

A crowd of 44,753 had attended the first leg at Anfield when Sterling equalised in the 59th minute, after Eden Hazard had given Chelsea a first-half lead from the penalty spot. 'It's now all to play for', said Gerrard, who added, 'We have to score and if we do, who knows what might happen on the night. It will be a tough game nevertheless, but we are confident … we always are.'

En route to the semi-finals, Liverpool had ousted Middlesbrough 14-13 in a thrilling and record-breaking penalty shoot-out (after a 2-2 draw), Swansea City 2-1 and AFC Bournemouth 3-1. Chelsea had knocked out Bolton Wanderers 2-1, Shrewsbury Town 2-1 and Derby County 3-1.

Chelsea (4-2-3-1): Courtois, Ivanovic, Zouma, Terry, Luis (Azpilicueta), Matic, Fabregas (Ramires), Willian (Drogba), Oscar, Hazard, Costa.
Liverpool (3-4-2-1): Mignolet, Can, Skrtel, Sakho (Johnson), Markovic (Balotelli), Lucas, Henderson, Moreno (Lambert), Gerrard, Coutinho, Sterling.
Attendance: 40,659

The second leg in South West London proved to be a right old bruising contest that went into extra-time. Reporter Neil Ashton wrote in the *Daily Mail*, 'The teams spat and snarled at each other all night' and it was, in truth, a real blood and thunder encounter that kicked off big time in the 12th minute when Chelsea's striker Diego Costa put his studs on the ankle of Liverpool defender Emre Can – an offence for which he should have been sent off. Former referee Graham Poll had no doubts, saying, 'That was violent conduct by Costa.' Also, Martin Skrtel and Costa clashed after the Liverpool centre-back appeared to bring down the Spaniard inside the penalty area halfway through the first half. The same pair then had a second argy-bargy in the 54th minute when Skrtel retaliated by swinging his boot at Costa, who had stamped on his foot. All good stuff.

Later in the game, in the 102nd minute in fact, Costa wrapped his arms round Gerrard's body and once again he could and should have seen red. The Liverpool skipper exploded with annoyance, a scuffle ensued and in the end out-of-depth referee Michael Oliver cautioned both Gerrard and Costa. There had been a few hesitant attacks before the first dust-up involving Costa and Can and as time ticked by Chelsea began to dominate possession, but Coutinho and Sterling always looked threatening when on the ball.

After a 17th minute slip by Kurt Zouma (who had replaced Gary Cahill), Sterling broke clear but was held up by John Terry, allowing Zouma to make up for his mistake by clearing the danger. 10 minutes later Gerrard drilled a sublime long pass out to Moreno, whose low shot produced an excellent save by the diving Thibaut Courtois, who soon afterwards dealt with a snap shot from Coutinho.

Chelsea lost Fabregas on 50 minutes (injured) and after that it turned out to be a fairly even second half when both Hazard and Costa went close for Chelsea and Gerrard, Sterling and Markovic likewise for Liverpool. 4 minutes into extra time came the game's only goal – a body blow for Liverpool! Willian's free-kick from the right was met full on by right-back Branislav Ivanovic, whose header flew past Mignolet like a rocket. Unfortunately it seemed as if substitute Balotelli should have been marking the scorer, but he 'lost his man' and it proved fatal.

5 minutes later Henderson should have equalised, missing with a free header from Sterling's cross.

Although they dictated the last quarter of an hour, Brendan Rodgers' side couldn't breach the tightly-knit home defence and in the end Chelsea squeezed through to the final 2-1 on aggregate and at the same time made it seven games undefeated against Liverpool, who had certainly given it their best shot. They had played at full throttle, engines roaring, but it wasn't enough and Gerrard left the pitch, head bowed along with his teammates. Chelsea then met London rivals Tottenham Hotspur in the final at Wembley.

What They Said About Stevie G

PELE – formerly of Santos, New York Cosmos and Brazil: 'Gerrard was an excellent player, absolutely world class. If I was a manager, everywhere I went I would have bought Steven Gerrard. He is what Brazil would want, because he always looked forward and has a big heart. I saw him play in Tokyo in a game against Sao Paulo. I said at the time, he is a great player. To me he was one of the best midfielders in the world – an excellent player.'

BRENDAN RODGERS, his last manager at Anfield: 'It is almost an impossible task to find the words to appropriately sum up Steven Gerrard and his importance to Liverpool. This is an era where the word "legend" is vastly overused, but in his case it actually doesn't do him justice. He is the best player I have ever worked with.'

ZINEDINE ZIDANE, former midfielder with Real Madrid and France: When asked if Steven was the best in the world, he replied: 'He might not have got the attention of Messi and Ronaldo but, yes, I think he just might have been. If you don't have a player like him, who was the engine room, it can affect the whole team. He had great passing ability, could tackle and scored goals, but most importantly, he gave the players around him confidence and belief. You can't learn that – players like him are just born with that presence.'

DANIELE DE ROSSI, Italian midfielder, in 2014: 'Gerrard has been my idol for ten years and is one of the best players in the world. He is the example of what all midfield players aspire to. He is always there in the heat of the battle, leading by example. He is everywhere you look – in defence, in the middle of the pitch and in attack. I would love to be close to that level.'

GARY NEVILLE, former Manchester United and England right-back: 'Steven was (is) undoubtedly a world-class player. I wish he'd played for United. One day, when we were together in a hotel, I asked him to come and play for Sir Alex Ferguson, telling him that the fans will take to you in no time. He just laughed, saying: "I'll do it, if you go to Anfield."'

RONALD KOEMAN, Southampton manager, 2014: 'If he hadn't chosen to go to America, I would have signed him for Saints. I am serious. He is a fantastic football player, really, at the top level.'

PATRICK VIEIRA, ex-Arsenal, Manchester City and France: 'The best midfielder in the game, I would say Steven Gerrard was. I really rated him as a player and as a man. I think he'll always be one of the best. He was powerful and strong, could attack and defend and he could score goals.'

KAKÁ, ex-Real Madrid, AC Milan and Brazil: 'England has always had individually strong players and I was a huge fan of Stevie Gerrard. He had the heart of a lion and was the icon of the modern footballer with his ability to attack and defend so well. He was one of the world's most complete modern players.'

THIERRY HENRY, ex-Arsenal and France striker: 'For me, and I have always said this, he will be regarded as one of the greatest midfielders ever. No doubt. The guy always put his foot in, always scored goals and did what he had to do to make his team win. That is what football is all about. He, for me, was Liverpool.'

SIR ALEX FERGUSON, long-serving Manchester United manager: 'Steven became the most influential player in England, bar none. I think that he did more for his team than anyone else, and had way more to his game. I watched him quite a lot. To me, he was Roy Keane. Everywhere the ball went, he seemed to be there. He had that unbelievable energy, desire, determination. Anyone would love to have Steven Gerrard in their team.'

CARLO ANCELOTTI, manager of Parma, Chelsea, Paris St German, Juventus, AC Milan and Real Madrid: 'Gerrard was a great player – undoubtedly one of the best midfielders in the world.'

PEPE REINA, ex-goalkeeper with Liverpool, Barcelona and Spain: 'Stevie was the badge of this football club, the soul of this team. Just by the fact that he was on the pitch was an inspiration for us. He always led by example and everything he did, he did with passion and a lot of commitment. He was a born winner.'

JAMIE REDKNAPP, ex-Tottenham Hotspur, Liverpool and England midfielder: 'Stevie G will go down as one of Britain's and Liverpool's all-time greats. He was just an incredible footballer and I had so many great memories of watching him play. He was Superman on the pitch. I wish I could have played with him more. It would have been a joy. He'll go down as one of the greats; there's no two ways about it.'

RONALDINHO, former Brazilian midfielder: 'For me, in the position he played, Steven was one of the very best in the world. For the job he performed, for me he was one of the greatest.'

RAFAEL BENÍTEZ, ex-Liverpool manager: 'Steven changed Cup games against Olympiakos in 2004, AC Milan in 2005 and West Ham in 2006. I think he was one of the best, if not the best, for sure.'

DANIEL STURRIDGE, Liverpool colleague: 'Steven will go down in history as one of the game's best-ever midfielders. He is just unbelievable every day, every game … the perfect example for the young player.'

GERARD HOULLIER, former Liverpool manager: 'Steven is a kind-hearted, generous person … a great personality. He made a lot of sacrifices and I wouldn't be surprised that one day he returned to Anfield as manager.'

RAHEEM STERLING, Anfield teammate: 'He has been brilliant to me. He always looked after me, always checked to see whether I was all right. He was an inspiration and great captain.'

GARY LINEKER, ex-England striker: 'Steven is one of the finest players to have graced the Premiership. He was a top, top player.'

PETER CROUCH, former Liverpool striker: 'I have been fortunate to play with many top players during my career, but Stevie G is easily the best.'

JOHN ALDRIDGE, former Liverpool striker: 'I always knew Steven was going to be a star. I've been watching Liverpool for fifty years and he is the best player I've ever seen in a red shirt.'

GRAEME SOUNESS, ex-Reds captain: 'Steven would get into any team anywhere in the world. A brilliant footballer.'

MICHAEL OWEN, former Anfield team-mate: 'It was a privilege to play alongside Steve. He has undoubtedly earned his status as a true footballing legend.'

RAY HOUGHTON, former midfielder: 'Steven has been a fantastic servant to Liverpool. He played through some of the tough times as well as good ones, and to go on season after season, producing brilliant performances, shows his true character. He was first class.'

KENNY DALGLISH, ex-Liverpool player and manager: 'Steven has made a massive contribution to the club for a very long time and that is why he is revered on Merseyside and beyond. Liverpool were lucky to have such a great player for so long.'

JORDAN HENDERSON, Liverpool playing colleague: 'The lads could go to Steven with anything and he would always help them out and put them first. With the aura that he had, he could be a different person but he was very humble as well.'

MARIO BALOTELLI, Italian international and Anfield teammate: 'Wow, I think of Steven as being at the same level as Andrea Pirlo. He had vision and technique, but was also powerful as well. He could do anything – an amazing player.'

BRAD FRIEDEL, former Blackburn Rovers, Aston Villa, Tottenham Hotspur and USA goalkeeper: 'I would think so many people in the city of Liverpool looked up to Steven Gerrard. He was an absolute true gentleman. I was happy to see that he never jumped ship and left Anfield when he had so many offers ... that was the mark of a true athlete, when a home-grown talent can stay and persevere with one club. He will go down as one of Liverpool's all-time greats, there's no question about that. His talent, his work rate, his endeavour and his leadership qualities made him a special player. He had everything.'

SVEN GORAN ERIKSSON, England manager (on naming him as his country's captain): 'On the pitch he was a fantastic footballer.'

JOEY BARTON, ex-Manchester City, Olympique Marseille, Newcastle United and QPR midfielder: 'Steven was probably as gifted a player as there has ever been in the Premier League, if not Europe, if not the world. He was at the top of the tree. He had everything. He was very, very difficult to play against and that's the reason I regarded him highly in the world of football.'

JAMIE CARRAGHER: former Liverpool teammate: 'Istanbul 2005 and what he did twelve months later in Cardiff would be my moments to savour. I couldn't split those two. And I'd have say he was the greatest players ever to play for Liverpool – joint first with Kenny Dalglish. So many times in his career he pulled us (Liverpool) out of the mire. Without him, how many trophies would we have won in the last 10 years?'

HARRY KEWELL, former Leeds United, Liverpool and Australian international: 'Steven was one of those players who was a born leader. It was great playing with him. He always produced something in a game. Whenever you were down you could look to him, he was always running hard, shooting hard, tackling hard. He always gave players inspiration to go and give their best. He was just a great player, up there with the greatest players ever to wear the red of Liverpool.'

DIDI HAMANN, ex-Liverpool playing colleague: 'The club has been fortunate to produce a lot of world-class players and Stevie is right up there with them. His contribution to the club was absolutely outstanding. He had all the ingredients of a top-class player – a great touch, passing ability, could score goals, was dynamic and had the talent to beat people, which not many have got. His all-round game made him one of the best players in Europe for six or seven years.'

JOHN BISHOP, comedian: 'Perhaps the best player ever to play for Liverpool, definitely the most influential, is Steven Gerrard. His work rate, commitment and desire to win, and his sense of responsibility, was second to none. He played for the supporters. He was there to give something back. He felt it when Liverpool won win and when they lost.'

RICKY HATTON, former champion boxer: 'Every club in the Premier League would love to have seen Steven Gerrard wearing their shirt. He's done what he's done on the pitch, he's captained his country. A big-time player with a massive talent, how can you not like someone like Steven Gerrard? There was one thing about him and that was the passion he showed on the pitch – somebody with that attitude. I have no doubt he would have been a good boxer. He's four feet taller than me so I'd have to bob and weave to get close to him.'

DJ SPOONY, Radio DJ: 'Stevie G is a very humble man. I thought that when I first met him when he was eighteen. I thought, here's a special player who respects his profession. He was brilliant at what he did. He's got to be one of the top three best Liverpool players of all-time.'

Did You Know?

The son of a garden fencer, Steven scored his first goal as a six-year-old playing with his pals on a field on the Bluebell Estate in Huyton.

Steve's first ever visit to Anfield was with his father in November 1986, to watch Liverpool beat Coventry City 3-1 in a 4th round League Cup replay.

As a young schoolboy Steven suffered from Osgood-Schlatter's disease – a bone condition that meant he was seldom fit for more than a week at a time. Things were to change dramatically as he got older.

Steven celebrated his 21st birthday with England at their training camp at the La Manga sports complex in Spain.

When he tried to nutmeg Paul Gascoigne in a Premiership game, Steven was slapped on the back of the head by his boyhood hero who said 'start behaving'.

Steven was booked as early as the 47th second of Liverpool 1-0 Premiership win over Manchester United in January 2002 for a foul on Ryan Giggs.

Steven broke the fifth metatarsal bone in his left foot during the 2-1 Premiership defeat by Manchester United in September 2004. He was sidelined for two months.

When he returned to action after that foot injury, a crowd of 6,280 packed into Telford United's Buck's Head Ground in Shropshire to see Steven play for Liverpool reserves against Wolves reserves.

Steven says the two best goals he ever scored in first-class competitions was his 30-yard rocket which bulged the net against Middlesbrough at Anfield in a Premiership game in April 2005. Liverpool, trailing to a first-half strike from Slizard Nemeth, were facing their 15th defeat of the season in the race when he switched the ball to his right foot and, facing the centre of the goal, let fly with a boomer into the top corner of Brad Jones' net. Aussie international Jones would join Liverpool in 2010.

His second best goal – although regarded by many as his best – was the brilliant 35-yard drive against West Ham United in the 2006 FA Cup final.

A proposed move to Chelsea in 2004 never materialized, as it was understood that the London club's offer of £32 million had been turned down by the Liverpool board.

Spanish giants Real Madrid were set to launch a £20 million player-plus-cash deal and a weekly wage of £150,000 for Steven in 2004. They wanted him to team up with Michael Owen and David Beckham. Nothing materialised.

Stevie G missed England's international match against Portugal in February 2004 to be with his partner (future wife) Alex Curran as she gave birth to their baby daughter, Lilly-Ella.

The most disappointing results (of many) were as follows: Liverpool's 2-0 home defeat to Celtic in the UEFA Cup in March 2003 (to go out of the competition 3-1 on aggregate); succumbing 4-0 in a Premier League game against Manchester United at Old Trafford the very next month; losing 2-0 at home to Chelsea in the vital Premiership game in April 2014; and drawing 1-1 at home with FC Basle in their final Champions League final group game of the 2014/15 season to crash out of the competition.

Steven has always looked after his elder brother Paul and his parents, Paul senior and Julie. Steven said: 'I've got one brother and I will never let him work. If the boot was on the other foot, I'm sure he would look after me.'

Steve's taste in music goes from Phil Collins to Coldplay; among his favourite TV programmes is *The Office*; his best film (until recently) was *Scarface* and his choice of restaurant is The Warehouse Brassiere in Southport. He's been going there for years!

It is believed that Steven and his wife earned £800,000 when they sold their wedding rights to *OK!* magazine.

Sponsorship

Steven Gerrard has had several different sponsorships during the course of his career, including deals with Adidas, Jaguar Cars, Xbox One and Lucozade. In 2014, *Forbes* listed his combined income from salaries, bonuses and off-field earnings at $17.2 million (£11 million) for the previous twelve months.

While Gerrard has worn several pairs of 'designer' football boots during his career, his first were supplied by Nike for his Liverpool debut, but he quickly signed a deal with Adidas in 1998 and since then has gone on to appear in a number of Adidas commercials with the likes of Zinedine Zidane, David Beckham, Lionel Messi and Kaká. Gerrard has worn ten versions of the Adidas Predator boot with the Accelerator being the first, and throughout his career he has been one of the brand's major boot endorsees. In 2013, Gerrard switched to wearing the Nitrocharge 1.0 boot, first wearing a pair in the League Cup encounter with Manchester United on 25 September of that year.

Outside Football

A practising Catholic, Steven and his wife, Alex, married in a Catholic ceremony in Wymondham on 16 June 2007. Apart from bother Paul, he has a cousin – Anthony Gerrard – who now plays for Huddersfield Town. Steven and Alex now have three daughters – Lexie (born in 2006) and Lourdes (born in 2011), the sisters of Lily-Ella.

Steve's autobiography, ghost written by Henry Winter, was published in September 2006 and went on to win the Sports Book of the Year honour at the British Book Awards. The autobiography ends with the words: 'I play for Jon-Paul'... Steven's cousin, who was tragically killed, aged ten in the 1989 Hillsborough disaster when Steven was only eight. Jon-Paul was the youngest of the ninety-six victims of that tragedy.

On 1 October 2007, Steven was involved in a low-speed road accident in Southport when the car he was driving hit a ten-year-old cyclist, who had inadvertently crossed Gerrard's path. Steven later visited the boy in the hospital and presented him with a pair of boots signed by Wayne Rooney, the boy's favourite player, after which he stayed to sign autographs for other young patients.

Councillors of Knowsley voted to make Steven a Freeman of the borough on 13 December 2007, two weeks before he became an MBE. He also received an honorary fellowship from Liverpool John Moores University in July 2008 as recognition for his contribution to sport.

In 2011, Steven appeared in the film *Will*, which was all about an orphaned young Liverpool fan who hitch-hikes to the 2005 UEFA Champions League final. Also in 2011, Gerrard established the *Steven Gerrard Foundation* in 2011 with the aim of supporting children's charities in Merseyside and beyond. Finally, in August 2014, Stevie G participated in the ALS Association's Ice Bucket Challenge with Cardiff City winger Craig Noone.